RESTORATIVE

PARENTING

7 WAYS TO TRANSFORM
THE PARENT-CHILD RELATIONSHIP

BY JOHN EHRHART

Profundity Publishing
P.O. Box 930, Erie, CO 80516

ISBN 978-0-9909600-0-3

www.restorativeparenting.com

To my children, Ian, Will, Jack and Grace, for providing me with the inspiration to create, and to my wife, Peggy, for not only the inspiration but the shared motivation and commitment to see our creations blossom and thrive.

It isn't simple responsibility which must be learned; rather, each youth must learn to respond to an innate spirit already burning inside. Each child grows around an indelible inner expectation that one day they will learn who they are to be in this world. The wound that comes to each person turns out to be the place from which a sense of individual meaning and purpose can grow. One of the responsibilities of those who would rule, lead, or mentor involves learning to see into the wounded areas of youth and spot the blessed streak that can be shaped into genuine discernment and healthy self-awareness.

Michael Meade, The Water of Life[1]

TABLE OF CONTENTS

INTRODUCTION

My exploration of the field of Restorative Parenting began ten years ago at an eight-day wilderness retreat in the high-plains desert of southern Wyoming. On the second day of my three-day, solo fast, I was lying on the ground, on my back, in the midst of a sprinkling rain, staring into the sky. I tossed out a question in the hope of finding some clarity in my life – "What should I be doing with my life?" Like many, I was seeking meaning and purpose in my life – I was trying to find my life path and choose my direction. As soon as the question occurred to me, I noticed the clouds start to take form. Amorphous perhaps, but for me they fashioned an image of two large nurturing hands cradling the earth, an image that soon transformed into a peace symbol. I responded with apprehension: "So I should create world peace?" and the peace symbol seemed to transform into an egg, which symbolized, for me, the need to *plant seeds* for world peace.

While this is a tall order, and one that may even seem quite esoteric or even futile, I knew exactly what it meant. The process of planting seeds for a peaceful world is one I see as a reflection of nature itself, although I have often lacked a sense of skillful means and conviction to engage it. In the desert, I had an opportunity to glimpse something beyond myself. I saw a place where my own conscious faculties did not limit me. I saw something beyond my limited conception of myself at work in the universe, a force that wills itself through nature. The peace sign was, for me at that moment a manifestation of this will. My exposure to the bare wilderness, devoid of my habitual life, acted as a point of inception from which I could see the world and my place in it from a fresh, innocent and vulnerable perspective.

There is a natural womb in each of us that nurtures the possibility of a peaceful world, one which can serve as an inherent source of wisdom, and one from which the manifestation of peace can spring. Peace is not an idea or a cause; rather, it is a capital-R Reality, the nucleus of the true self, and realizing this individually may well be the path toward a more peaceful family and a more peaceful world. As the Dalai Lama has said, *"Although attempting to bring about world peace through the internal transformation of individuals is difficult, it is the only way."*[2] And peace and relationship work within the family is the next step.

Restorative Parenting does not advocate any particular style or school of parenting, nor is it critical of any particular parenting method. With possible exceptions, one parenting style is no better or more right than another. All styles are right styles – we all parent from a place that feels right to us. We do not have to feel as if we have failed by not reading the so-called "scientific research" or by not sending our kids to the "top" schools.

Scientific interest in correct parenting methodology has been around – in one form or another – probably about as long as science itself, yet we are all still faced with the same difficulties and trials that parents have encountered throughout history, problems which are mostly relationship-based. Technique and theory might help form the facade of our parenting styles, but it is relationship building that fuels the heart and soul of what it means to be a parent. We are all coming from the same foundation of love and compassion – our intentions are pure and most of us just need some tools to strengthen or rebuild the connections that seem to be missing – the connections that lead not to any so-called "ideal" family life, but rather simply to increased understanding and respect.

What Restorative Parenting intends to do is to help support your preferred style and to do so in a way that cultivates secure attachments, healthy development, and a capacity for working with the wounds that inevitably arise from family life. Rather than allow such injuries to cause us to feel lost and alienated, we instead utilize them to live more fully and bring our individual and collective gifts to the family, the community, and the world at large.

The world is not in short supply of parents who believe they know everything there is to know about how to raise a child correctly – but what is in short supply are parents who have the ability to "not know" – to be curious, from moment to moment, about the dynamic truths we all confront -- truths which are not available in any book, but which present themselves willingly if we are able to let go of what we think we know and open ourselves to what shows up in the moment.

Restorative Parenting grew in many respects out of my desire to make the most out of my less-than-perfect performance as a parent. As a facilitator and mediator in various Restorative Justice programs, I have had the privilege to participate in a powerful community process that enables both criminal offenders and victims of crime to give voice to their stories, recognize and take responsibility, as applicable, for the harms of crime, find a way together to help repair those harms, and, finally, through a redemptive journey that extends from those acts, to reintegrate offenders back into the community -- in the end both more whole and more prepared to be of service to the world.

Although the notion of Restorative Justice in the criminal context lies far from the focus of this book, it is perhaps worth noting that, as in the world of parenting, the criminal justice system very often reinforces harmful behavior on the part of offenders, and alienates victims in a way that leaves them feeling empty and voiceless. Those within the wider governmental system, the prisons, law enforcement, and the courts – collectively acting as authoritarian surrogate parents of anyone thrown into the system -- know that what they are doing is not working, yet continue to prosecute, sentence and advance new punitive laws that only perpetuate the cycle of violence and alienation.

Although less extreme in the short term, very similar systemic problems are encountered in the context of parenting. We parents confront the same frustrations as we threaten, ground and shame our children for breaking household rules. We know that it doesn't work, that it often only makes things worse, and we feel the same type of alienation and voicelessness that many crime victims feel. Yet by the same token, we also find moments where our children reach out to us and we explain to them that we love them dearly and only want the best for them, but sometimes only to return to an unconscious habitual state in which we continue the cycle of harm and alienation.

In this book, I will speak directly to the origins of this dysfunction and to a variety of ways that we can move out of this frustrating place. My intent is not to judge any parenting habits or to claim that there exists some miracle cure for the frustrations and emotional pain that inevitably accompany the parenting experience.

Rather, my goal is to offer insights and practices (many adapted from proven techniques of mindfulness, meditation, Eastern philosophy and Western psychology) that can help build the honesty and trust needed to strengthen the parent-child relationship and to heal the wounds of childhood, or as Michael Meade says, to "see into the wounded areas of youth and spot the blessed streak that can be shaped into genuine discernment and healthy self-awareness[3]."

"We are, by nature, allergic to coercion."
Gordon Neufeld, Hold on to Your Kids

Chapter 1

ATTACHMENT

Attachment is the foundation upon which the seven transformative ways of Restorative Parenting are built. It represents the mechanics of the parent-child relationship. We are attracted to those we are attached to and happy to be of service to them.

Perhaps that's why when my wife asks me to do something for her, I immediately stop what I am doing and give her request my full attention. Well, not always, but if there has been a strong history of reinforcing the attachment components of our relationship by staying connected at a heart level, my agreement to her requests becomes automatic, and vice-versa. When negative responses occur, such expressions are simply feedback to us that our attachment may be weaker than the ideal.

This applies to our children as well. Whenever one of my children exhibits signs of anti-social behavior or becomes more demanding and confrontational, or, for that matter, withdrawn and non-communicative, it is often the direct result of a lack of warmth and heart contact in the relationship. Such symptoms can be attributed to both the quantity and quality of our togetherness, but I have found that if I simply focus my attention on that child and engage them in a consistent and continuous way, day after day, those symptoms tend to clear.

I remember my first discovery of this phenomenon with my son Will, when he was 5 years old. Not long after the birth of his little brother, he started expressing himself in negative and seemingly destructive ways. I decided that I would spend an hour or so with him alone after work. One day we started wrestling for fun, and after that he would come up to me after I got home and say, "Dad – it's time to wrestle." So we wrestled almost every day for an extended period and his mood and interpersonal demeanor changed dramatically and in a stable way.

We have to be creative with such engagements and adapt them to the apparent needs of the individual in the moment (for instance, my wife Peggy presumably would not like it were I to start a wrestling match in response to our own relationship problems!), but the fundamental relationship issues will always come back to the depth of the attachment. Are we in heart-centered contact with each other? Do we trust and work to understand each other?

This is of course true of all of our relationships. Attachment is really the actual expression of our affection for our children on a regular basis. In my experience, children do not know that we love them unless we show them, with our time and attention, that we love them.

This notion is not merely a platitude, but rather has grown out of the ideas of some of the central figures in the science of child development. For example, we can reflect that the major achievement of a child in the preoperational stage of Piaget's child development model (as will be discussed in greater detail in the next Chapter) is that of *object permanency*. This skill is represented by the ability to know that an object still exists even if it cannot be seen (and explains why the "peek-a-boo" game is so engaging to a child entering this stage). Although this cognitive skill is routinely acquired by developing babies, it is not called "object" permanence by accident – in other words, it does not extend to non-objective, emotional data.

Indeed, the term "permanence" is likewise no accident. Rather, for children, love is a temporary and transitional emotion -- for that matter, even for adults emotional constancy often does not occur outside of the parent-child relationship. When it does, it is represented in the form of archetypal religious or political figures such as Jesus Christ, the Buddha, Gandhi, Mother Theresa, and Martin Luther King, Jr. It is represented only by those very select few who transcend the normal human relationships that the rest of us struggle with on a daily basis. To most of us, the idea of loving our enemy, for instance, is frankly ludicrous, much less loving the person who merely irritates us at work. Even for the sages, opening the heart and transcending such defense mechanisms is a daily practice that brings great challenges.

The famed writer Charles Bukowski called love "a dog from hell" in recognition of the endless emotional suffering that seems to accompany it. With this in mind, if we are to assume only an enlightened sage can achieve emotional constancy, then our children certainly will not be conscious of the underlying stability of their emotional connection to us, or automatically recognize continuously that our love for them is both unconditional and unlimited.

So we must do the hard but rewarding work of forming, strengthening and reinforcing our emotional connections to our children on a daily basis so that they are continuously exposed to our universal love for them and our commitment to do our best. Accordingly, the central focus of this book will be to present and discuss strategies to do this work effectively, and to explore proven philosophical and experiential support systems for these perspectives.

Holding Environment[4]

When we were born, we were weak and helpless (and, if we are to believe our grandmothers, extremely cute!). From the outset, we were held and supported in one way or another. Our survival depended on it. We were held, and the environment in which we were held had a lasting impact on our psyches and our souls, an impact that remains with us now and for the rest of our lives. Although this impact is largely unconscious, it influences the perspective we have of our current environment and it reveals itself in both our physical and verbal expressions.

When the "holding environment" is calm, nurturing and intact, we feel relaxed and in tune with our surroundings. We feel as if everything is okay and that it will continue to be okay. However, when significant disruptions occur, we become thrown out of that sense of security and can lose our trust in ourselves, the people around us, the world, and the universe. Yet, these disruptions are not all bad. They represent a challenge or trial to which we must respond and, in the best circumstances, overcome.

How we learn to respond to these disruptions determines, in large part, our resilience and capacity to mature and grow as individuals. So by working through such disruptions in a way that reinforces our sense of dignity and well-being in the world, we strengthen the foundation of our world view from one of suspicion and fear to one of openness and trust. We feel that we can relax and life seems easier.

If the environment we were in as infants nurtured our physical and emotional states and needs, it likewise contributed to our sense of trust that the world would provide for us. However, regardless of the extent to which our mothers and fathers provided an attentive and loving cradle, there were also disruptions to the trust we experienced in relationship to our world, and the memories of those disruptions became embedded in our psyches. The impact of such disruptions also became bound to our neural wiring and our personal consciousnesses, which in turn influence every aspect of our perceptions and behaviors.

Our instinctual response is inevitably to attempt to create a perfect holding environment, avoiding all disruptions, which although a noble exercise, is ultimately futile -- what a friend of mine once referred to as "crazy making". The attempt to create this optimal environment is exactly the way our ego (our constructed yet false "self") attempts to make itself "safe" in response to our negative experiences as children, and hold us to an impossible standard.

It is simply the reactivity of our own defense mechanisms at work, all the while supporting and strengthening this erroneous self, one which is grounded not in authenticity but in mere personality. While it is likely that a positive loving holding environment does indeed correlate with a more psychologically well adjusted life, the infant is further impacted not only by his or her physical environment, but also by the psychological and emotional states of the mother and all other caretakers. In short, you cannot create a perfect environment and even if you could, it would come with its own set of side effects, so what else is there?

The holding environment is obviously an essential aspect of the parent-child attachment process throughout the lives of both children and adults. It represents the underlying ground from which we perceive and interact in the world. Additionally, a critical component of that environment is the skill with which we handle and process the numerous disruptions among our experiences.

We might also be tempted to blame ourselves for any dysfunction present in our family lives. This too is a way that the ego (and perhaps the superego, our internal judge, as well in this case) reacts to any threat to its very limited view of reality. The truth is that if there are no disruptions and conflict, there will be no development or growth. Indeed, it is the very disruption to our attachments that encourages the deeper development of the attachments themselves.

My sixteen-year-old recently changed high schools, at our request, which was a major disruption due to his strong resistance to the idea. In the next chapter, I will speak about brain science as it relates to development, but I found out in the last couple of years that there is no objective scientific knowledge that could have prepared me for the alternate reality from which teenagers periodically perceive the world. When I came up against it in this case, I tried to reason with him and pushed back hard against his vitriol and exaggerated defenses, which only hardened his position. This created a wall of miscommunication between us that felt unbreakable at the time. He felt unheard and disrespected, and the only way he knew to respond to it was with the language at his immediate disposal. After realizing this, I made a vow to simply mirror back his concerns during our next conversation, and I found that the more I did this, the more he was open to hearing me. The point is that I was able to learn from the disruption and spontaneously create the tools I needed to strengthen our connection.

The disruptions experienced by our children -- often initiated by our flawed parenting – can actually (and thankfully) serve as the vehicles for the eventual realization of their true selves. Because of the natural will to grow, our relationships, if healthy and authentic, will always be in flux, and when we are aware and mindful we have the capacity to flux and flow with it. Through our own practice in confronting these challenges, we have an opportunity to coach our children in how to hold a more dynamic view of relationships and reality.

We can practice with our child the ways of recognizing and speaking to such disruptions. The more we can see objectively, with flexibility, what is happening, the more responsibility, and therefore power, we have to guide our own perceptions in a way that returns us to a relaxed state – namely, the natural true state of being held, which is a fundamental aspect of our being, regardless of how the outside world has treated us.

In short, we can give them this truth. We need not tell our children how *we* are interpreting *their* experience – rather, we simply hold open the space for them to talk about it, and ask open-ended questions in order to foster their curiosity about their experience or, perhaps in more childlike terms, "how it feels" in their hearts, minds, and bodies. In so doing, we promote their physical, emotional, relational, and spiritual intelligence.

My own memory of early childhood puts me in a very loving and nurturing holding space with my mother. Of course there were obvious disruptions and distractions to that environment, particularly in my case as the sixth of seven children with my younger sister having been born before my second birthday. There was enough chaos in that house to crush any dream of a perfect holding environment than I ever could have hoped for as a newborn.

Many years later, when my mother died, my grief went back to that place with the thought that the source of my bliss on this earth was now gone. Yet, upon deeper reflection, it struck me that the holding environment that represented the bliss of my early childhood originated not solely in my mother's arms, but rather in the simple ground of being that holds us all, here and now. My mother was the vehicle of that nurturing love, not a singular source. While the self-loathing I feel from my perception of her disapproval at times may come and go, the fundamental trust and secure holding are permanent.

This realization reinforced for me that we cannot build a perfect environment for our children -- we can only make ourselves available as vehicles of love to our kids, and reassure them that they are loved unconditionally and infinitely. Our job is not to make sure they never feel pain or difficulty, but rather to create an environment that makes it safe to navigate all of their experiences, whatever those experiences happen to be. They can then feel safe enough to answer the questions "What does that feel like, and what does that mean, to me?" We can set the stage for a life grounded in trust – trust in themselves and their own curiosity.

Developing the skill to look inward for safety and trust sets children up to deal effectively with the pressures of their social lives as they mature. As pre-teens and teenagers, they become increasingly influenced by their peers, by marketing through advertisement, and by a host of fearful messages aimed at them from every direction. Yet, developing a deeper relationship with a secure holding environment, one that is grounded in their sense of being, can enable them to orient their locus of control internally. They can then learn to recognize that the messages they are receiving from the outside (both good and bad), as well as the emotional reactions they have to those messages, do not represent the truth of who they are.

Unconditional Love

When I was in my early twenties, my mother tried to relate to me how she loved her seven children unconditionally and how the unconditional part is really and truly unconditional – that there was nothing we could ever do to harm the depth of her love for us. Being just out of college with degrees in psychology and philosophy, and also being -- as many in their twenties see themselves – "smarter" than anyone else on the planet, I loved to both argue any point, even on such inscrutable notions as unconditional love. I first joked that I could see how her point could be true with *me*, but that she really couldn't love my little sister that way. Then I decided to take the position that there was no such thing as unconditional love and that love as a concept is conditional on its face. My mother had, I suggested, chosen to love us over others simply by virtue of our birth.

I thought I was pretty smart, but my mother knew me better than anyone and would forgive me my folly and ignorance faster than anyone, so rather than try to argue with me, she simply smiled and appreciated both my presence and folly in a way that gently demonstrated the experience of unconditional love. She showed that it is impossible to explain it – that you must experience it to know it. And although I was unable to construct a logical explanation for it, I was able to receive her unspoken message in a way that helped me to understand, over time, the deeper truth for myself.

When we claim, as parents, to love our children unconditionally, we are expressing a truth (and a feeling) realized in our highest state. Yet when it comes down to it, we still can react with disgust and disappointment when our kids don't live up to our expectations – expectations that in more honest moments, we realize that we often failed to live up to ourselves as children. Unconditional love is not a declaration requiring no reflection. It is not a platitude. Rather it is at bottom a spiritual practice that requires discipline and effort.

When our children engage in behavior that is reprehensible to us, our first thought is often (and sometimes borne in anger) to jump to the question of how they should be punished. The feeling that we love them is always there, but we fool ourselves into thinking in moments of blind frustration that punishment and so-called "tough love" is actually a means of expressing our love. This justification, I would argue, comes from our lowest selves. We could respond, alternatively, by first looking at the strong emotions that may have overcome us in the heat of the situation at hand.

When we look at our emotions closely and really allow ourselves to feel them directly – paying specific attention to how they feel physically -- we are granted insight and inherent wisdom that might escape us otherwise. We can inquire into the origin of the immediate emotions and realize that they come from somewhere within *us* and are not "caused" by our children.

We can then reclaim our role in the relationship and come from a place of true unconditional love – imperturbable love. We can get back in relationship with our son or daughter and be interested in finding out what their experience is – and we can do this because we are not caught up in our own self-perpetuating reactions. It is with this in mind that further discussions of restorative responses to problem behaviors will be addressed throughout this book.

Dependence and Independence

My son Jack, at seven years old, gets up in the morning, showers, dresses, brushes his teeth, and politely asks for breakfast. He is not a freak of nature, but he is our third child and has learned that life is just easier when he does things for himself. Thankfully, this independence has come very naturally for him and it does for most children. I could further encourage his independence and show him how to make his own breakfast. He would probably run with it -- he even now will often figure it out and get a bowl of cereal if help is not forthcoming.

However, putting the breakfast routine solely on his shoulders would remove one of the most crucial (and rewarding) aspects of attachment from our relationship. That he still depends on me for part of his morning routine creates an attachment-forming opportunity, one through which he is informed and reinforced in a tangible way about his sense of security in the world. It tells him that if he needs me, I will be there for him, and, in a broader sense, if he needs anyone, someone will be there for him.

The core and unconscious belief structure that he turns to here (one stored in his limbic system according to neuro-anatomists) tells him that he will be safe and cared for no matter what happens. If I were to take the position that he should do everything to get himself ready, that he should be able to make his own breakfast, and that he shouldn't be bothering me while I'm dealing with his younger sister's seemingly endless list of needs, he would be pushed to an alternate core belief that he is on his own, and that if he asks for help, it won't be there. Faced with this, chances are he would be drawn to stop reaching out altogether.

Many of us parents hold to this same core assumption ourselves and may still believe that it is an accurate way of perceiving the world. That said, it must be noted that even as adults our minds are very playful and malleable, and we all have learned, through our own development, that perception all too often precedes and defines what we take to be reality.

The practice of developing a secure attachment encourages dependence in children, especially when it is answered in a loving, nurturing and generous way. Yet, we do not want our kids to be so dependent on us that they are unable to help themselves. On the contrary, we rightly set limits on dependence and help them develop a healthy sense of confidence that they can take care of themselves when they need to. We want to encourage self-reliance and self-confidence, although we also want them to know, deep down, that we are there for them, and it is through our daily interactions and by simply being there for them when they ask that they will learn how the world is, and from a psychological perspective, gain an understanding that how they perceive the world is how the world ends up being.

We must come to terms with the fact that our children will eventually be independent adults and that we are here to support the development of their independent personalities and to encourage the adult qualities that are meaningful to us. Our job is not simply to allow them to use us as servants until it's time to go. Rather, it is to help them form meaningful, authentic, intelligent, and dynamic human connections that will translate into strong and sustainable loving relationships and communities of their own.

Dependence and Essence

Dependence on the part of our children generates attachment through our ability to meet their physical, emotional, and psychological needs. Attachment disorders, as defined in traditional psychological diagnoses, often arise out of disruptions in the course of meeting such needs.

The attachments we form as adults, however, come from an adult place, and are not as typically grounded by obligation or dependence as with children. The attachments we develop with our children and with other adults are grounded in our simple presence and compassion in the present moment. I will talk a lot in this book about what represents a truly empowered adult perspective, and this notion is a fundamental component of that perspective. Here, the fully realized potential of all adult relationships happens free from expectations with respect to the other person and from a place of dignified vulnerability and openness to receive the other person as they present themselves currently, as opposed to how we expect them to behave.

Our children above all deserve the benefit of this mature perspective – a perspective that does not constantly label them as predictable and consistent in their personalities, before they themselves even have a chance to mature. The greatest gift that we can give to our children is that of reflecting before them, not their personality, but their true selves -- before, after, and beyond personality and personal judgment, a reflection grounded in pure Being.

This is the self that we as parents should know better than anyone, because it has been there from the very beginning, and although a personality has surfaced and obscures it to varying degrees, this true self, this essence has not gone anywhere. It is the self that we greet, in curiosity and wonder, every time we engage with our children.

For many years, I facilitated meditation classes at a maximum security juvenile detention center, and I heard stories from many of these young people that revealed common themes including abandonment, physical and sexual abuse, parental drug and alcohol abuse, and parental imprisonment. These kids had been shaped in many ways by these often horrific histories, yet they never failed to shine, at one time or another, with the light of their true selves, and I always felt fortunate to meet them in that light.

A truly empowered adult perspective also originates from a place of non-dependence on our own part. It is fully autonomous in relation to others. It recognizes that we act within the relationship from a place of complete personal accountability. Although we may have needs ourselves that are pressing and urgent, we do not place the responsibility for getting those needs met on any individual.

Rather, we might freely seek help in skillful ways that allow us get our own needs met, but we remain, at bottom, solely responsible for our needs and we know it as the truth. The inspirational quality of this sense of autonomy is that, from the truly adult perspective, rather than alienating us from others, our autonomy is what makes authentic connections possible. We recognize that we must practice to maintain a skillful and authentic presence in our relationships for our needs to be met in a meaningful way.

Note on practice sections: As made clear throughout this book, the art of being a parent – the art of being a human being – is essentially the art of being aware. The conflicting messages bombarding our daily lives from every direction possible (our mind, our body, our emotions, our loved ones, and the outside world at large) confuse the situation and make it more difficult to be and act from a place that feels real. The practices that are presented at the end of each chapter are opportunities for us to develop our awareness and our capacity for presence and equanimity when we need them most. It is often the time when we most need our strength and self confidence that they seem to abandon us. Practicing being in touch with these qualities on a regular basis will help us realize that they haven't actually betrayed us and that we can make them more accessible during these vulnerable times.

PRACTICE: Loving-Kindness (Metta) Practice

Regardless of the amount of love we received growing up, we are now in a position where we must begin to provide *ourselves* with the love we need, and with this very simple practice, we have a way to do that. One of the biggest obstacles to our own development and a truly empowered adult perspective is the resentment we harbor towards others. This practice gives us a way to do the very difficult work of confronting these barriers. And, finally, it gives us a way to honor the full potential of our highest moral perspective, which includes all beings.

Using the four mantras, repeat the lines in unison with your breathing, "May I be safe, May I be happy, May I be healthy, May I be at ease" until there is a sense of absorption with the mantra. Then, expanding the mantra, replace the word "I" with the name of a specific loved one for whom you feel a deep bond (e.g., "May Sally be safe..."). Then expand the mantra to a neutral person with whom you are acquainted and for whom you feel no strong feelings. Then expand the mantra to a person with whom you have difficulty – this person can range from a family member with whom you are currently having a disagreement, to someone who has committed a crime or other injury against you. Then expand the practice to include "all beings".

In sum, apply the mantra to the self, a loved one, a neutral person, an enemy, and, finally, all beings:

May all beings be safe.

May all beings be happy.

May all beings be healthy.

May all beings be at ease.

"In fact, at this point in history, the most radical, pervasive, and earth-shaking transformation would occur simply if everybody truly evolved to a mature, rational, and responsible ego, capable of freely participating in the open exchange of mutual self-esteem. There is the "edge of history." There would be a real New Age."[5]

Ken Wilber

Chapter 2

DEVELOPMENT

We are put on this earth to develop. Our development potential is not only inherent to our biology; it is also the seed of our happiness. However, many of our personality structures are set up to make us fear the prospects of development and change, so we end up suppressing the very engine of our contentment.

Fortunately (yet, sometimes, unfortunately) the prospect of continued self-realization is an unceasing impulse, one that persists in knocking on the doors of our lives until we answer it. The more we suppress this impulse in order to mute the knocking, the more we suffer and the more we become blinded to the reality of our true being.

A child's development is rapid, natural and encouraged by those around him or her, but only to a point. As soon as children reach a stage of development that seems to mirror (or, "worse" yet, surpass) that of the general population, the encouragement for further growth wanes, sometimes even reversing to the point of discouragement. Thus, there emerges at higher stages of development an unconscious and seemingly collusive conspiracy to undermine and even halt the continued expansion of our consciousness.

Regardless of our own histories concerning personal development, it is incumbent upon us not only to encourage the ongoing development of our children throughout childhood, but also to impart to them the value and art of continued lifetime growth. We can achieve this through modeling and promoting a healthy curiosity about the nature of our experiences in the moment. We repeatedly ask "why?", and we maintain a strong sense of our physical responses as life happens around us. A few such simple skills can take us through the span of a lifetime.

In this chapter, we will explore this process of child and adult development in more detail, briefly consider a developmentally based approach to parenting, and look at several supportive structures that can be implemented into the lives of our children. First, however, we will consider two fundamental trajectories of development and the obstacles inherent within them.

Transformation

Evolving development along a continuum of growth requires an individual to dis-identify with their current level, to opt instead to identify with a higher perspective, and then to integrate the lower perspective into their current view. As adults we may do this perhaps two or three times in our entire adult lives. In contrast, children transition through a minimum of five or six major developmental stages from birth to the age of twenty, which of course implies that they are repeatedly dis-identifying with who they are and redefining themselves on a regular basis.

While we as adults are busy solidifying our perspectives, they are constantly (and often happily) shredding theirs to pieces. So I cannot overemphasize the need to be gentle with yourself and with them as they develop.

The philosopher and developmental psychologist Ken Wilber uses phrases such as "transcend and include" and "expand and embrace" to define this integral process. As we grow and expand our perspectives, we integrate and honor where we have been before. As parents, we seek to support -- both in ourselves and our children – a process of opening from a narrow identity to one of expanded awareness and acceptance.

Translation

Development can occur horizontally, vertically, or both. The development process does not necessarily require a perpetual climb up a ladder of stages; rather, we can also become more fully aware and grounded at the stage where we currently reside. One of the things we can seek to do is to support our children where they are by encouraging a healthy translation of their current level of development. In order to do this it is helpful to have a sense for their "center of gravity"[6] on the developmental spectrum.

We can also go back and work on lower levels. This is something I have on occasion found the need to do while coaching for my kids' sports teams. Like many adults, some of my own experiences in sports while growing up were somewhat wounding psychologically, and when my children started to play it all came back to me as I was forced to re-confront the uncomfortable feelings I had experienced in order to integrate them into my current self.

This work is necessary not only for the parent but also for the child. In order to properly support children in their sports experiences our own development as parents must be ongoing as well. Because we cannot perceive from a higher level than the one where we actually reside, continued vertical development is crucial. As we develop vertically, we can appreciate the increased insight and confidence that comes with the process, as well as the decreased levels of fear and anxiety. With this we can recognize that such development is fundamental and support it not only in our children but in everyone we meet.

Pathology

Pathology invariably occurs to some degree as we adapt to our developmental environment. To the extent that we fail to integrate the disruptions of our childhood experiences, our personalities become negatively influenced by unconscious pathological forces. On the other hand, from a very early age we develop defense mechanisms and survival strategies that assist us in navigating the world yet which simultaneously block us from seeing the world clearly. This double-edged sword can lead either to stable functioning in the world or to dysfunctional neuroses that hinder and obscure our development.

Development should be aimed toward an ever-widening perspective and increasing inclusion, but we are too often plagued by anxiety and self-doubt as a result of the instinctive reactivity so typically learned in early childhood. This is the reason that psychotherapeutic methods so often seek to drill down to childhood memories of the mother and father as a means to unearth these initiatory responses. The goal is to bring these responses to light in an attempt to integrate them into the current self, so that they might have less of an unconscious influence on our state of mind.

The Case for Parental Development

The pioneering psychologist Jean Piaget defined four stages of cognitive development that have become the foundation for numerous developmental theories regarding the progression of cognition in children through adolescence. Briefly, they are:

Sensorimotor Stage

0 to 2 - Children develop simple reflexes, the ability to repeat physical actions, hand-eye coordination, curiosity, and the ability to use primitive symbols. They develop the ability to know that an object is present even though it is hidden from the senses.

Preoperational Stage

2 to 7 years of age – This stage is exemplified by a strong sense of egocentrism. Children cannot take the perspective of others, and cannot distinguish between their perspective and that of others. Children can now think in symbolic terms, giving them the capacity for

pretend play. They also engage in magical thinking, which they use to explain their world. As they progress through this stage they become very curious about why things are the way they are, revealing the emergence of primitive reasoning.

Concrete Operations Stage

7 to about 12 – At this stage, children begin to distinguish between their perceptions and the perceptions of others. They develop an increased ability to focus on more than one aspect of a stimulus making them better problem solvers. They have the ability to think logically about what's happening. They have not yet developed the capacity for abstract thought.

Formal Operations Stage

12 and beyond – Children develop a more abstract view of the world. They are capable of hypothetical and deductive reasoning, increasing their understanding of scientific and mathematical concepts. The ability to see multiple perspectives and consider multiple outcomes, gives them the capacity to understand consequences of their actions. The ability to form their own views of the world also emerges at this stage.

Each of the four stages encompasses significant achievements in cognitive capacities, culminating in an aptitude for abstract thought and what we generally think of as adult perception.

As a culture, we pay close attention to children as they progress through these stages. Doctors, teachers and school counselors will track these capacities, as defined by Piaget, through the school years, and will raise concerns if these milestones are not being met.

After we have reached the formal operations stage, however, the careful consideration of development is often simply put to the wayside. We finish school, get jobs and support ourselves. As adults we often seek equilibrium and comfort, whereas change and transformation will be forced upon us only when we encounter problems in navigating our personal and professional relationships. This state of affairs refers us back to the value of confronting and integrating prior wounding experiences, so as to bring us to higher levels of perception and increased resourcefulness for life and all of its servings.

The truth is that there are further stages of development that represent intellectual, moral, artistic and spiritual achievement through our adult lives. Over the past thirty years, there has been a great deal of research by researchers such as Abraham Maslow, Erik Erikson, Clare Graves, Jane Lovinger, Lawrence Kohlberg, Carol Gilligan, and James Fowler to name just a few, documenting the higher stages of adult development and most of the findings are quite consistent regarding the important characteristics necessary for us to continue along our never-ending road of maturation.

Clare Graves, one of the pioneering theorists in matters regarding higher stages of adult development, and whose research led to the foundations of the development of Spiral Dynamics[7], has laid out one of the most coherent models of adult developmental psychology.

Graves focuses on the importance of evolving our world views and expanding our perspectives along a developmental trajectory that culminates in what are referred to as "second tier" stages in which increased capacities for perspective and integration, and an existence focused on subsistence, become referenced to being. This second tier is marked particularly by an expanded appreciation for the gifts and capacities of previous developmental achievements, decreased levels of fear and anxiety, and a reduced tendency to over-identify with core beliefs and traditional cultural roles. This is really where the potential for an enlightened life emerges.

As we summon the moral courage to face our fears and challenges to our egos as they present themselves, we are cyclically called to live from a higher place. In the process, we are often prompted to go against what we have long believed and even to abandon what we once held sacred. We are beckoned to gradually thin our egos and live from a place that is wiser and more dexterous in the face of chaos and change. And it is these qualities of perception that will serve our children as they trek up the mountain of development, as they look not for declarations about what is right and wrong, but rather for understanding and appreciation of both their struggles and the gifts they bear.

Moral Compass

We often think of morality in terms of right and wrong or good and evil. While these dichotomies are quite useful for story telling, movie making, and dream interpretation, they are insufficient to the work of deciphering the complex ground of relative perspective in which we live on a daily basis. Politics as it plays out on our global, national, and local stages engages this divisive language in order to persuade and achieve objectives by any and all means.

One side might have us believe that a vote for itself is a vote for "morality." In view of the known effectiveness of this otherwise low-brow strategy, we rarely witness truly high-minded debates -- debates in which the needs of all are honored, on issues that are central to not only our daily lives but also our survival as an evolving species. It is much easier to pull someone down than to pull them up, and this is the predicament we face with regard to both our development as a people and our development as individuals.

The pioneering developmental psychologists mentioned previously contributed some of the most extensive research data on the question of how we develop morally. The central idea is that we develop along a moral line that gradually increases in its care and concern for all. We start out as deeply egocentric, focused on our own survival and meeting our own needs. Yet as we increase in our moral intelligence and capacity, we gradually expand our sphere of concern to our family, friends, team, school, community, country and so on.

We can look at history and be disheartened by what we see from a moral perspective, but we can also see a gradual moral expansion in ourselves over time, and if we are lucky our children will achieve a moral perspective that we never dreamed of. Further along still, we look to their future descendants to develop new ways to meet the needs of others that will make our own interpersonal communication seem stone-aged in comparison. For now, however, we can only teach our children to respect others and to practice taking the perspective of others in every situation. The golden rule still stands as the model for morality in the world. Meet all others' needs as if they were your own – to paraphrase.

Brain Development

With regard to children, not only do they not see things as we do, they are neither developmentally nor physically capable of seeing things from our perspective or even understanding certain perspectives. Through the adolescent years, the area of the brain that governs planning and decision making (primarily the frontal cortex) and a key area believed to be involved in problem solving (the corpus callosum) are still undergoing dramatic growth.

Medical imaging studies have suggested that teenagers are still relying greatly on a part of the brain responsible for reactionary gut responses (the amygdala) to interpret emotional information, rather than using higher-level thinking parts as adults tend to do. Keeping this in mind will help us communicate to children on their level. While they are yet not capable of rising to our perspective, we adults by contrast do have the ability to imagine what they might be going through if we keep in mind their particular developmental stage and remember back to the typical milestones, strengths and challenges that go along with it.

Through engaging in practices that prioritize relationships and promote personal accountability, we can contribute to the proper wiring of the brains of our children and help them make decisions that do the same.

Integral Restorative Parenting

Restorative Parenting represents an integral approach to parenting where all impacting perspectives and values are honored and the full range of influencing paradigms is considered. The goal is to arrive at a more transpersonal approach to raising our kids, ourselves, our community, and our species toward both an ever-expanding developmental context and an increasingly sustainable framework.

By "transpersonal approach," I am alluding to the possibility that we can transcend our personal identities, worldviews and prejudices in favor of an alternate approach that recognizes our limitations and strives for a more open and evolved structure. We realize that we are not at the end of our developmental evolution and, as such, we are continuously opening ourselves up to higher perspectives and potentials.

The integral model developed by philosopher and psychologist Ken Wilber emphasizes the so-called AQAL (pronounced "aqual") framework, which ambitiously references all quadrants, all levels, all lines, all states, and all types, as will be touched on further below.[8] I will attempt to briefly demonstrate how Restorative Parenting covers these dimensions and also how Restorative Parenting might add qualities to the discussion of what an integral parent is. Since my intent is to focus directly on the heart of the Restorative Parenting philosophy, I must necessarily leave detailed explanations of integral theory to Ken Wilber and his Integral Institute.[9]

Integral parenting references a perspectival approach to parenting. Around the age of 12, we gain the developmental capacity to take another's point of view, yet many of us rarely ever use this skill. The core idea is that if we can take a first, second and third person view of a situation, then we are more likely to perceive it in a more holistic way and therefore respond more effectively.

The *integral quadrants* represent an intention to be aware of and pay attention to 1) the individual subjective perspective, 2) the individual objective perspective, 3) the collective subjective perspective, and 4) the collective objective perspective of the reality we are presented with. In other words, the perspectives of the individual, relationships, community, objective scientific inquiry, and cultural and organic systems, as well as their inter-relational significance, are all taken into account.

Levels are simply stages of development as discussed previously concerning our general path of fundamental childhood development and our continued maturation through adulthood. Consideration of this component is obviously essential to our parenting effort, regarding both the developmental health of our children and ourselves as autonomous beings and as models of living for them.

Lines refers to the specific and subtle categories of development along which we progress independently of our cognition. For example, psychologist Howard Garner[10] developed the theory of multiple intelligences, which reveals our tendency to be good at some things and not so good at others. Some of his "lines" include: Verbal/Linguistic, Logical/Mathematical, Visual/Spacial,

Musical/Rhythmic, Bodily, Kinesthetic, Naturalist, Intrapersonal, and Existential.

States refers to the myriad states of consciousness that permeate our human experience, including gross states, subtle states, and causal states, which can be associated with waking states, dreaming states, and dreamless deep sleep states. Interestingly, the brain waves associated with dreamless deep sleep states are very similar to the brain waves exhibited by those sages thought to represent enlightened waking perspectives, which implies that each night, when we go to sleep, we cycle through enlightened states of consciousness, from infancy on[11].

The final component of the aqual model, *Types*, invokes a capacity to discriminate, objectively, the variety of influences associated with subtle differences. Personality types as defined by the Myers-Briggs model and the Anneagram model reveal fascinating behavioral tendencies based on where one falls in the model.

The significance of this to Restorative Parenting is that we are expanding and opening our perspectives to receive truth as it comes in rather than forcing our version of the truth on the situation. Truth is something that we try to become open to, rather than something we already know – so the suggestion is that parenting at the highest levels happens in the *now*.

We are not carrying around the answers in a brief case, but are rather improvising them, in the moment, based on the information that presents itself. This is what makes parenting a truly ongoing *practice* – we practice being fully present in all situations so that we can promote our highest ideals in any given moment.

This is not to say that already existing data is not valuable. Part of the integral art is to skillfully apply known information to the inquiry at hand. Nevertheless, regardless of what statistical or observable information we may or may not possess at the outset, successful parenting occurs when we are open, vulnerable and tuned in to what is being presented in the moment.

When we practice this, we are practicing parenting – otherwise, we are simply making automatic cyclical references to the same outdated and superseded ideas that otherwise threaten to make our relationships stagnant and lifeless. Relationships thrive when they are fed, and they eat soulful presence for breakfast, lunch and dinner. We must appreciate how important our relationships with our children truly are and feed those relationships three meals a day every day for them to truly live.

By applying Wilber's AQAL framework to our approach, we adopt an intention to be integrally informed. This does not mean that we are perfectly informed, but rather that we are open to receiving new information from different perspectives and therefore to growing our own. The approach is for know-it-alls and non-know-it-alls alike. Integral is -- by definition – nonexclusive.

Nature as a Contributing Factor to Wholeness

I recently experienced the frustration that often typifies the chaos that can sometimes pepper our household at a child's bed time. There are several ways -- some that are better than others – in which I tend to address these instances and attempt to regain some of the resourcefulness necessary for good parenting in the face of such conflicts.

One is to separate myself from the situation and try to ignore it. Another is to simply react directly to every request, demand or expression – to just push through the situation with sheer will, and hope that the aggression that can accompany a lack of patience does not take over. Another – and more effective -- method is to stop and try to resource myself with breathing and mindfulness practice. All of these methods are quite common for me, depending on how conscious or unconscious I happen to be in the moment -- the more unconscious I am, the more difficult it is to get perspective on the situation.

In this particular episode, I just stepped out onto the back porch and sat down looking out over the landscape, breathing in the night air and connecting with the outside world with all of my senses. A short time later, my 2-year-old followed me out and quietly sat on my lap. When I reentered the house with my now quiet toddler, I felt like a completely different person – as if the fragmented parts of my being (physical, mental and spiritual) had just been fused back together and I was whole again, or at least much more whole than I was only minutes before.

In retrospect, I am now reminded of an observation made by American naturalist and author John Muir, who, commenting on the deep nexus between the natural world and a person's inner life stated: "I only went out for a walk, and finally concluded to stay out till sundown, for going out, I found, was really going in."[12]

One profound truth that never ceases to amaze me in its apparent lack of logic, yet seemingly consistent confirmation, is that when we change our perspective, we change our world. This is why when I first created the web site for Restorative Parenting, the first thing I put on the front page was something a trusted teacher once said at the beginning of a class: "Our intention is not to change the landscape, but to learn to see with new eyes." You can indeed put Humpty Dumpty back together again and interacting with nature can help.

At the close of that bedtime experience, the situation in the house had completely shifted and I was able to engage with my children in a healthier way -- ending with me reading the same book to all four of them in the same room, without incident -- a rarity -- and they all went peacefully to bed. Really.

If the simple act of stepping outside and relating directly with the natural world that happens to present itself to us in the moment can transform a situation like that, there seems to me little doubt that one of the most important gifts that we can give our children is the gift of nature. Few deeper benefits can be imparted than to educate them about the natural world, to spend time with them in it, to model for them the ways to relate to and respect it, and to recognize the integral part it plays in our survival as a species.

Wilderness Rites of Passage

My son Ian was about to enter his freshman year of high school, and leading up to this important life moment I felt strongly that we should honor the transition and reinforce for him both the security of his attachments and his emerging sense of autonomy. This new sense of autonomy in an adolescent, particularly when buttressed by a communal support system, brings with it confidence in decision-making. It brings also an organic moral compass which, although it may be influenced by those the child is attached to, is confirmed only by personal experience and reflection.

We notified my son's wider support system that we would be marking this rite of passage with a wilderness trip, and involved the men in his life in the process. As adults, one of our key responsibilities is to assist the adolescents in our lives in their passage to adulthood. If we do not, their passage may well by guided by forces that do not have their best interests at heart.

On the second day of our trip to the wilderness, Ian departed on his solo time, where he spent time alone as a practice in autonomously relating to nature and to his inner personal guide, the essential friend on his life journey.

While hiking along a mountain trail, he encountered an old man who asked him if he was with anyone. When he responded that he was alone, the man remarked, "They don't make kids as tough as you these days". Here in the middle of a sparsely populated wilderness, at 11,000 feet near the Continental Divide, appeared a wise elder who reflected back to my son the fact of his essential inner strength, the very important innate quality that will serve him on the arduous trek he now faces.

We might tend to think of an encounter like this as coincidental and insignificant, but the importance of the manner in which the deeper truths of his autonomy were spontaneously revealed to him cannot be overstated. This encounter can be seen as a sacred space within the context of the ceremony he was engaged in, where all encounters and experiences are significant, and represent direct communications from and to the soul. This *transpersonal* context is the lens through which we can directly perceive the truth of how spirit participates in our development.

Transpersonal Psychology, a core discipline underlying Restorative Parenting, is similarly a study of the psyche in all of its mysterious yet knowable wonder. It seeks to integrate the whole potential of human experience and understanding into the science of the healing arts. It is comfortable with ambiguity and strives to transcend and integrate the paradoxes of the dualistic mind through contemplative and experiential means. It recognizes spirituality as an influential force in personality development and, perhaps most of all, stands as a living inquiry that is open to the unfolding infinite well of learning that is the privilege of our human existence.

The importance of spirit in the application of Transpersonal Psychology cannot be overstated in that it is this element that, when awakened, allows us to find value and meaning in our own lives and the lives of others. Ritual initiation of adolescents into the adult stages of life represents a seamless example of how the integration of and connection to spirit can mark a life transition, and in so doing can further promote and define a qualitative developmental pattern for life.

Meditation – Ritual – Council Practice

The process of integrating the peak experiences associated with wilderness rites of passage relies on practices such as meditation, ritual and council practice.

Meditation allows the individual to process elements of his or her identity in a way that promotes self-transcendence. Ritual honors the process of initiation by infusing it with a sacred dimension. Council practice, as described in detail in Chapter 6 , promotes respect and communication within community. All three practices generate an opportunity to encounter states of consciousness that promote a realization of one's lack of separateness from the natural world and the rest of existence, which in turn can lead to higher levels of moral and spiritual development.

The ritual of initiation into adulthood can be seen as a specific task under the larger societal responsibility of mentoring. Mentoring seeks to expose the gifts of each young person and to support the development of these gifts for the greater good of the community. Mentoring young people into adulthood is one of the most meaningful and important things we can do as adults. It is one of our primary responsibility, as adults - to pull children and adolescents up the primordial ladder of maturation, and it is our job regardless of whose children they are.

Malidoma Somé, a West African author with a deep background in initiation retreats, contends that every individual contains a genius that represents a particular communication from the "Other World," a gift that is meant to benefit the community. Somé also observes: "The mentor perceives a presence knocking at a door within the pupil, and accepts the tasks of finding, or becoming, the key that opens the door". [13]

Such ideas remain at the heart of our developmental process and apply at all stages of life. The approach of recognizing the inherent goodness and gift of each person -- speaking to it and acting on it -- echoes the deepest meaning of our lives and our place in the world.

Enlightened activism may thus be inspired through initiation rituals by opening up the initiate's sense of connectedness to the world and concern about it as a concern for the self. By integrating and supporting such experiences, we pave the path to engagement with the world.

By way of an example of a situation that involved a relative lack of the initiation experience, I can turn to my own experience after my father died when I was ten years old. I had three older brothers who were all there for me in different ways and contributed greatly to my own maturation. I believe, nevertheless, that a formal initiation ritual combined with informed wisdom-based mentoring would have enhanced my own transition into adulthood. In attempting to seek my own truths in the absence of more formal initiation experiences, I went through a period of adolescent drug experimentation, something fairly typical among my peers of that era, yet what I further suspect may have been grounded largely in a desire for the initiation and sense of meaning I craved so deeply. Predictably, I found only further chaos and dysfunction in terms of my relationship to the world.

Yet, with a more formalized initiation process, particularly under the mentorship of caring adults, the promise of a genuinely transformative result is well within reach. As the Brothers Grimm observed long ago in their tale "Iron John": "When the wild man had once more reached the dark forest, he took the boy down from his shoulder, and said to him, "Thou wilt never see thy father and mother again, but I will keep thee with me, and I have compassion on thee... Of treasure and gold I have enough, and more than anyone in the world."[14]

The Creative Process

The creative process is one through which children encounter initial inspiration, the challenges and disappointment of dealing with obstacles, and the emergence of new intelligence as a result of perseverance and trust. The process that generates a work of art is the same process that creates continuing individuation and developmental progress.

When we learn a song on an instrument, for example, we become inspired at the beginning and envision ourselves playing the song and impressing all of our friends. Yet soon we must truly start learning it and confronting the struggle that comes with training ourselves, mentally and physically, to remember the motions necessary to play the notes and chords in succession. This is typically the point at which we either give up completely or commit fully to learning the song.

Only after we have overcome the various potential crises of self-doubt, boredom, frustration, and the like, can we expand into a level of familiarity and earned relationship with the piece of music we are trying to master. All of this conditions the brain to appreciate things that do not come easily and to tolerate the ambiguity and chaos that are inherent to the process. We learn that when chaos arises, all is not lost, and that hidden beyond the confusion is a place where vision becomes reality. When Nietzsche observed that what does not kill us makes us stronger, he was referring to this truth – that chaos, darkness and suffering hold within them the seeds of strength, power and intelligence.

This life skill is essential in developing an inner life – one in which we relate to ourselves in a way that is independent of outside influences and opinions -- yet a skill that will ultimately find application to our outside relationships as well. The creative process – one beginning with an internal focus but with a product that is ultimately shared with the community – is thus also a relationship process. When we teach our children the value of this process as it applies to all of our life activities, the chaos becomes a light even in the face of challenges or emotional wounds that may arise in the act of creation itself.

PRACTICE: Nature Meditation

Nature is an important contributing factor to our sense of wholeness. It has the power to reliably bring us and our children back to what it truly means to *be present,* which is our most important resource as a developing adult and as a parent.

Instruction: Although this is an outdoor exercise, it of course does not require a pristine wilderness, flowing ravines and expanses of natural beauty, etc. All you really need is the sky. Go outside and find a spot where you can be relatively alone, and select an object in nature – it could be the sky, a tree, a flower, a weed, or a single blade of grass. Clear your mind completely of all expectations and prior knowledge about what this object is, what its usefulness is, and any of your ordinary assumptions about it. Pay attention to your breath -- on the out breath, let go of these assumptions, and on the in-breath simply be with the object. Do this for 10 minutes and afterward reflect on and write about your experience if you are inspired to do so.

"You can't make your kids do anything. All you can do is make them wish they had. And then, they will make you wish you hadn't made them wish they had."[15]
Marshall Rosenberg

Chapter 3

EMPATHY

We are set up, as parents, to mess up our jobs terribly, and there really is very little we can do about it. It is written in the myths of the ages that fathers, regardless of their noble intentions, will unknowingly either devour or reject their sons. In many cultures, fathers are not even included in the adulthood rites of passage of their own sons, and likewise with mothers and daughters. Here there may be too much potential for bad blood, or psychological projection, particularly where the authentic gifts of the children are to be brought into the light and given back to the community.

Parenting can be a wounding process that takes its toll on both the parents and the children, and the first thing we need to learn as parents is how to practice empathy for ourselves – the practice of self-empathy is simply the practice of being compassionate with ourselves in recognition and acknowledgment of our emotional experience in the moment. We may be feeling painful hurt feelings while engaging with our children, and the more we can be aware of them and be compassionate with ourselves in the midst of those feelings, the more present we can be.

My son, Will, has a gift for language. Words flow out of him in a largely unconscious, free flowing way. Sometimes they are what we might call "inappropriate". Sometimes he makes noises or sings whatever he is thinking, which likewise can be received as disrespectful by the family members around him. Most of the time, however, I view these behaviors simply as a creative exploration of vocal play. If he were a DJ, he might be nominated for a Grammy.

As far as I know, he generally only engages these impulses at home. He otherwise interacts in very "normal" ways in wider social situations, but when he is alone with our family, the impulse is set free. The way we respond to this from an interpersonal perspective is critical, and represents a good example of the importance of coming from a context of empathy, in that what we are hearing in terms of the literal words and what he is trying to express are often two totally different things.

There is often real value to be had when we stop responding to the naked words and simply feel into the heart and soul of the person we are attending to. Our thoughts and emotions can be like a blowing wind or a crashing ocean. Trying to nail down the intention of the wind is rightly viewed as insanity. Why are you blowing here today – now? Do you have a personal problem with me? No, it's just the wind blowing and there are any number of influences that contribute to why it blows at a certain time and place.

The point is that we are so much more than our words or even our thoughts, and if we can learn to feel into both the presence and the *being* of our children, rather than believing we have to correct everything they do, we will find they end up being much more connected to us and more likely to follow our example.

Yet it is one thing to suggest that we do this and another to actually do it. The starting point is to navigate the world of our unconscious responses and find ways to adapt to them, so that we might clear a path through the often painful world of reactivity.

Triggers as Barriers to Empathy

It's Sunday, and I'm sitting in my big comfy chair, enjoying a cool beverage, watching some TV, and my wife walks in the room and says, "So what are you going to do today?" Before I even realize it, I scowl and my shoulders move forward and tighten into my body. The first thing that comes to my mind is, "Watch TV, what does it look like?" Yet her question was totally harmless, and in itself presented no judgment or threat. Nevertheless, I respond as if I'm being attacked by a wolf in the wilderness, and all I have to defend myself is this lousy TV remote. What is it that evokes such a defensive response from such a harmless question?

First, it is useful to consider the neurological process that governs and initiates the triggered experience. Research by neuroscientist Joseph LeDoux[16],, as described by Daniel Goleman in his seminal work on emotional intelligence, demonstrated that the amygdala, the part of the brain typically associated with the primitive fight-or-flight response, plays a much larger role in governing emotional responses than had been previously thought.

When the amygdala associates a stimulus with fear, discomfort or hate, it immediately and often successfully tries to take over the brain, especially the rational, thinking parts of the brain (the neocortex and cortex). In short, it has a profound ability to exert an overriding influence on our reactions. Not only does it manage our fight-or-flight response, it can also -- by overriding the thinking parts of the brain -- initiate more complex knee-jerk reactions, including those that lead us to blame, rationalize, judge, defend, ridicule, yell, cry, scowl, etc.

The amygdala maintains an emotional memory storage box that goes back to infancy, when it was fully formed, but when the neocortex and cortex were not. In view of the infant's obliviousness to any true form of rationality, those emotional memories are limited to primitive, emergency-oriented emotions.

Yet, later in life, when a current situation even slightly resembles one of those memories, the amygdala interprets it through its own lens, and it does so before the higher brain even has a chance to figure out what's going on. Even after the neocortex and cortex have had some time to catch up, the amygdala continues to cloud our thinking in favor of its earlier, irrational response.

Triggers can appear in the form of specific words in a conversation, or they can be other noises, smells, certain objects, body language and subtle tones of voice. My triggered response to my wife may have had nothing to do with what she said, or even her perceived intentions, but rather some subtle stimulus that was also present: e.g., the tone of her voice, an expression on her face, or even the color of her shirt. Still, unless I am curious and mindful about where my knee-jerk reaction may be coming from, I will always be subject to it.

Although this may explain why we react to situations in ways that would otherwise be in conflict with our values and current level of development, it does not tell us how to regain control of our higher brain from the amygdala once the response has been initiated. While there is often little we can do to prevent a subtle trigger in the first place, there is something we can do about it once it occurs. Through practice, we can recognize when we are being triggered and employ tools that will both change the way we respond in triggered situations as well as strengthen the connections that enable our higher brains to play a more prominent role in our response, thereby making a truly intentional response more readily accessible over time.

As with all of our unconscious reactions, behaviors and decisions, the most important thing we can do in response is to sense into our experience and expand our awareness of what is happening. We start by recognizing the cues of being triggered.

Signs of being triggered include: *Physical Signs* -- breathing either too fast or too slow, a rapid heart rate, or muscle contraction or tension; *Thinking Signs* -- blaming and defensive thoughts, paranoid thoughts, judgments about yourself or others, a desire to punish, thoughts of revenge, or a desire to attack or flee; *Emotional Signs* – feelings of anger, hatred, resentment or fear; *Behavioral Signs* - saying things you don't mean, insults, sarcasm, screaming or yelling, door slamming, or a refusal to communicate at all.

Once we recognize that we are triggered, our response depends on the situation we are in. Regardless, we should not give in to the immediate impulse to react while we are in the middle of our triggered state. Rather, it is important to create space in a respectful way, sense into the present symptoms, and take steps to recover from the triggered state.

While the steps to recovery from a triggered state are obviously always individual and often intuitive, there are a variety of useful techniques that one may employ. For example, you can try taking deep breaths aimed toward the area of your body where you perceive the physical response to be located – consciously feel the air from your in-breath permeate the part of your body where the tension lies. What matters is what works for you, but the point remains that merely stopping to *consciously take a breath*, in the moment and regardless of anything else, may well allow you to effectively respond to the trigger.

Another possible technique is to move your body in a way that takes back your sense of power and strength. You can then re-enter the situation from a non-triggered place (as non-triggered as possible) and take an appropriate action, informed by your whole body, brain and mind, and not just by the reactive amygdala. This re-engagement step is an important one because, if we can do it from a non-triggered or less triggered place, we can retrain ourselves cognitively while lessening the impacts of resentment and similar repressive tendencies.

Maintaining an awareness-focused stance is another key to shifting our state quickly when triggered. Over time, we can effectively "reset" our cognitive responses in order to react from a more resourced place. Although recognizing and working with our triggers, especially at the outset of the trigger, may be seemingly impossible at times, consciously working to do so can create a safer, more harmonious home for everyone, while also limiting the influence of stress and its negative effects on our bodies and minds.

Recognizing the origins of our triggers is ultimately a function of awareness. Sometimes, regardless of our good intentions to meet such triggers with full awareness, we may find ourselves in the middle of a screaming match before we know what hit us. Yet, even in that sad and perhaps inevitable circumstance, finding ourselves there in whatever the moment brings is a key to developing the very awareness that we may have lacked in the same moment. What we do after is what defines restorative relationship work.

The discovery and observance of a trigger that we have reacted to, whether unconsciously or not, may often be followed by feelings of self-loathing or self-judgment. Yet, really, it should be a moment of celebration – knowing that we have seen our reactivity in action and now have another tool to repair any harm arising from that place.

The Shadow

The story of our development is inextricably linked to the values and beliefs we pick up as we navigate childhood. Some of these values and beliefs serve us throughout our lives, while others are discarded as we discover their limited usefulness. Many core beliefs are generated from positive experiences, including themes of trust, love and abundance, whereas others are inspired by negative experiences derived from a fearful perspective, including beliefs centered on scarcity, conflict, danger and low self-value.

It may be tempting to judge certain core beliefs as "bad and others as "good". From an objective and discerning perspective, if I could choose my core beliefs, I would of course opt for those that support happiness, safety, well-being, ease, harmony, belonging and connectedness.

Unfortunately, we do not have the privilege of choosing our core beliefs because they are adapted unconsciously from childhood psychological survival instincts, arising typically while under attack. They served to protect us from emotional pain when we were children, and despite their later lack of utility, they persist into adulthood and interfere with the potential to live a full life and be a whole person. The rub is that the more we cling to the seemingly "good" core beliefs, the more reinforcement we give to the so-called "bad" beliefs.

The monumental task of the adult is to gain an awareness of these beliefs and their origins, and to determine their usefulness in the present moment. Is my fear of rejection at parties useful to me? Here, poet and author Robert Bly[17] spoke of a "long bag" that we drag behind us, noting that we spend the first twenty years of our lives putting things in the bag and the next twenty trying to get them out again.

The essential task is to see what lies beneath a given core belief. For example, if I look more deeply at the overall experience of anxiety at parties, there may be a physical component consisting of a pain in the chest, or a feeling that the heart is constricted as with a vise. Sensing into such physical phenomena, I discover a deeper wound that I have carried with me since childhood, yet which paradoxically I am somehow trying to protect. Further still beneath that wound, I find a feeling of loss, deficiency, or inadequacy. Deeper still, I experience a spaciousness that is black and unsettling, but yet now is noticeably free of physical and emotional pain. That spaciousness then opens into a clear light, expansive and unlimited – yet also empty. Out of this emptiness there emerges a feeling of warmth, appreciation and love. I begin to see my true self, completely void of all beliefs, values, judgments and fears.

Discovering core beliefs and universal needs is a means to uncovering the true self. Just beneath these beliefs and needs are emptiness, essence and true nature. As all roads are said to lead to Rome, all useful teachings and exercises reflect this core truth. We are truly limitless beings and we -- in our essences -- need nothing because we are everything. The core beliefs, the processes and the teachings are simply signs that lead us to encounter the true self. This is Self-awareness.

Through careful observation of and subsequent dis-identification from our core beliefs, core values, and self-images, we can break free from the prison of our less deliberative perspectives. As we find ourselves outside, among the stars and the sky, a cool breeze blowing, we can see that the prison of a core belief is not our real home and that our sense of limitation was only in our minds.

How does this information and experience help us with empathy and parenting? Unless we are completely deluded, one thing that we realize quite early on as parents is that regardless of our good intentions, it is impossible to protect our children from encountering their own problems with core belief systems. Although we might hope that even if they will inevitably form these core beliefs, we can at least encourage those beliefs to be positive ones. While this is not a bad strategy, no matter how hard we work to reinforce positive belief systems and how diligently we try to protect our children from harm, we must accept that we are destined to fail in our efforts, and on occasion we will fail miserably.

Accordingly, it may be better to consider that when the Buddha declared his first noble truth – namely, that "Life is suffering" – he did not exclude the lives of children raised by so-called "perfect" parents. Not only are these core beliefs (and their attendant core wounds) inevitable, they are the grist of the mill for ego development and contain within them the embers that ignite life's passion and purpose. The better goal is to focus on teaching our children about false senses of limitation and to coach them on how to meet these limiting forces.

One of the things I do (or at least try to do) for my children is to simply create as much space as possible for them to communicate these beliefs, these wounds, and this shadow, but without forcing upon them my own analysis or judgment. I instead focus on helping them with the mindful practice of being aware of these challenges. This is one reason why I read monster stories to my kids. My daughter's preschool class spent a week on monsters. They read all kinds of books about monsters and did monster crafts in which they created monsters using a variety of media. Similarly, when my eldest son used to wake me up because he saw a monster, I had him describe it down to its most minute detail, and we would then draw it together. The more we defined it, the less of a threat it became. Do not shy away from listening deeply to your kids when they are ready to talk about difficult experiences, and be ready to listen without the need to "fix".

Both Sigmund Freud and Carl Jung taught that the key to psychological health was to make the unconscious conscious. The view is that by probing into our repressed material, and relating it to whatever our current trouble may be, we can resolve that trouble. This is the basis of most psycho-therapeutic practices to this day. The concept of shining a light on our shadow in order to heal and grow has far reaching implications with regard to our skillful adoption of restorative practices. By focusing these restorative practices on prior harms, we can take the events, decisions and lapses of judgment that might have otherwise remained repressed -- shoved into our bags never to be seen again -- and shine light on them in a way that offers the promises of health and growth.

By engaging in these practices on a regular basis and as a way of life, we can work through our core beliefs and shadow material as we move through life. In so doing, we can also model this approach for our kids and coach them in a way that will help them deal psychologically and emotionally with a fast-paced world that is so often lacking in empathy and authenticity.

Superego – Dealing with the Inner Critic

Freud delineated three main parts of the psychic self: the id, the ego, and the superego. According to Freud, the ego, which represents our personality (the conscious sense of self through which we interact with the world) balances the demands of the id (which is derived from our instinctual, impulsive, and largely pre-rational drives) against the demands of the superego (which in turn is often described as a "parental" voice of limitation and criticism). He defines the plight of the ego thusly: "The poor ego has a still harder time of it; it has to serve three harsh masters, and it has to do its best to reconcile the claims and demands of all three.... The three tyrants are the external world, the superego, and the   id."[18]

Until the age of 3 or 4, the superego has not yet begun formation. As we begin to experience the world as separate individuals, the superego emerges as a guide to living in the world in the midst of other individuals. It starts out as the voice of our primary caregivers -- telling us what we should and should not do -- only later transforming into an inner voice that stays with us for the rest of our lives. At some point in our developmental trajectory, however, the superego becomes superfluous and harmful to our progress. It ceases to be a correcting force and instead becomes limiting and coercive. We realize that it is a child's tool.

Psychologist A.H. Almaas, creator of the Diamond Approach to self-realization, has this to say about the superego: "From our perspective, the superego is the inner coercive agency that stands against the expansion of awareness and inner development, regardless of how mild or reasonable it becomes. It is a substitute, and a cruel one, for direct perception and knowledge. Inner development requires that, in time, there be no internal coercive agencies.   There will be, instead, inner regulation based on objective perception, understanding, and love."[19]

If we are to assume a truly empowered adult perspective, it is imperative that we recognize the presence of the superego and do what we can to push it out of the way of our experience. The method Almaas offers employs the acronym "RIDD":

Recognize the superego through presence of guilt, fear, praise or "should" messages;

Identify the specific attack, the content of the message, and who it sounds like (Mom, Dad, an older sibling, etc.);

Defend against attack with force until you...

Disengage and you are freed from its influence, now feeling stronger and more autonomous.

Certain distinctions may be helpful here as to the practice of defending against the superego. Actions of the superego are accompanied by both physical sensations and specific messages. So we must first distinguish between the physical sensations we experience and the messages we encounter. We *recognize* and *sense* the physical sensations and *defend* against the specific messages until we feel genuinely strong and supported.

If we pay attention to what's happening physically, we will typically notice an impulse to fight back against the superego's defeatist messages. You can engage this fighting impulse and embody the energy that accompanies it in our effort to defend by stomping your feet, clenching your fists, or punching the air -- all to demonstrate both the capacity to defend yourself and the realization that you are not helpless and do not have to identify with or believe the superego's messages.

Next, we must distinguish between our superego's symbolic embodiment (i.e., our actual mother, father, older sibling, etc.) and the superego itself. The superego itself is not a true person, but rather a superfluous and immature mental construct that impedes fully empowered adulthood. We must thus seek to identify the specific message and the associative source of that message in order to gain insight into its origins, so that we can set a clear boundary around it.

Yet, of course, we certainly need not and should not directly confront a poor, sick, dying mother to do this work. Rather, the goal is to simply defend in a clear and forceful way against the internal message, recognizing that our personality has constructed the message in a way that may look and sound like her through messages she occasionally conveyed to us when we were children.

I myself have a big, abusive, parenting superego, one which has created in my unconscious an "ideal" parent that is always fully resourced, always present, and always in right relationship with my kids – in other words, the fictional, enlightened and "perfect" parent. This is the parent with whom I am compared by my superego. Yet no human being can live up to this ideal. It is an ideal that is difficult to even describe, much less satisfy or closely approach, yet it tries to convince me that I am a terrible parent who fails again and again to live up to my own standards.

Yet, recognizing the falsity of the superego's message, I am in a place to realize that although I am not and can never be the "perfect" parent, it is still okay. I know I can only do my best with what I have in the moment, and in order to do that I know I must draw upon my true strength -- a strength which I now reclaim from the superego.

How do these developmental and psychological truths impact the ways we parent? One powerful realization, once we have witnessed first hand the incredibly negative impact that the superego can have on our own progress and self-image, is that we too become the very source and embodiment of that same junk-yard-dog superego for our kids.

So we can see now why we (and all children, past, present and future) at some point reject our parents in a forceful way, especially during adolescence and young adulthood. As such, much of this rebellion may be less of a true rejection of the parents themselves, but rather may better represent a natural, instinctive and healthy fight against the superego as loosely embodied by the parental voice.

Again, this is where self-empathy and empathy for our kids is so strongly needed. Those compulsive planners among us might try to think their way through the thicket, but we must remember that the process of developing a superego is unavoidable. We might also think that we can simply replace the superego's negative messages with positive ones – or, failing that, simply let our children run feral. Both of these may be interesting proposals, and seemingly worth a try, but the fact remains that the superego will continue to co-opt all of the "should" and "shouldn't" messages available in any system.

Rather, if there is one primary parenting technique that I consistently advocate, even against resistance, it is that we simply recognize that the superego is going to be there, notice how what we say (and how we say it) contributes to it as embodied by our own parenthood, and speak to these observations as plainly and honestly as possible. Will we occasionally make mistakes? Yes, of course we will, but we nevertheless have what we need to turn those mistakes into gold. We need simply to work at staying present and responding in the best ways we can -- maintaining always an appreciation for the truth, whatever it may be, and supporting that as a core family value.

In the end, it is difficult to underestimate the importance of teaching our kids how to work with the superego as they mature and reach stages where they can grasp its presence. Even with my 4-year-old daughter, Grace, I work to help her develop a healthy sense of her own power against the superego's perspective. When she is insulted or hurt by the judgments of others (and internalizing the same via her nascent superego), I try to help her acknowledge the hurt and allow her to see it. Then I ask her, "Who gets to say?"

She typically responds (if she has processed her feelings), "I do, Daddy." This practice of self-referencing gives her a little bit more power over her own self-image (here I am careful to coach her that not even Mom and Dad "get to say"), and as she matures she will be increasingly able to distinguish the central and balanced self who "gets to say" from the superego-self who offers only unhelpful, judgmental, and often hurtful things to say.

For my own part, I keep a red Wiffle Ball bat at home that I sometimes use to confront my superego (embodied in this exercise as a couch pillow). One day, I showed it to Grace and told her what I use it for. I asked her if she wanted to try it and she had a lot of fun smacking the pillow, saying, "I get to say!" and "No!" Now when she sees the bat, she asks for a turn.

In short, one of the most fundamental ways that the superego oppresses us is by co-opting our energy and strength. By swinging the bat and moving our bodies aggressively, both Grace and I have learned -- in the moment – to reclaim that energy and strength.

Requests vs. Demands

One of the most common coaching lessons I employ with my kids is to convey to them the value of communicating in terms of requests as opposed to demands. I suspect it is one of the simplest and most important teachings I will ever impart to them: If you pay close attention you will see just how common demands are in our daily communication. And, unfortunately, they are far more common in our communications with our kids than with others in our lives.

The distinction between requests and demands is often not so much about having good manners as it is about simply getting to the outcome we seek. We are far more likely to have success getting what we want with a request than with a demand. It is that simple.

Yet, the distinction is also about dignity, respect, and lessening the overall friction in our communications. Psychologist Marshall Rosenberg,[20] the creator of the Nonviolent Communication approach, has discussed an experiment which indicates the unconscious yet negative posture that parents often adopt in relating to their children. In the experiment, Rosenberg divided his parent-subjects into two groups, sent those groups into separate rooms, and instructed each to address a particular conflict scenario. For one group the conflict was with their children, and for the other it was with their neighbors.

When the two groups come back together, neither knowing the nature of the conflict that was assigned to the other group, the group whose conflict was with their children was described as being less respectful and compassionate. These results illustrate how, when in conflict with their children, parents often automatically assign less importance to respect, discretion and diplomatic discourse.

Deep Listening as a Means to Foster Empathy

Deep Listening is not a skill in which we use only our ears. When we practice deep listening, we utilize our entire being. It requires that we be fully present with all of our bodies, minds, and spirits. If we receive our children in this way, we will give them the greatest gift a parent can give to a child – the gift of being truly seen for who they are in the present moment. Once given, you will quickly see the impact of such a gift.

There are guidelines that we can call upon to deepen our listening and, as a result, our connections to our children. First, we can work to adopt an intention to listen without feeling a need to respond – in other words, trying not to start from the objective of imparting "appropriate advice". Dialogue is not the objective: Connection is. When we listen without an intention to respond, we minimize distraction and open our hearts to the speaker. In addition, by not offering up our usual well-meaning, well-reasoned and mature response, we free our child to be who they are without the fear of being judged or reprimanded for their thoughts, feelings or behavior.

Second, as we listen, we can work to focus part of our attention on our own bodily sensations. Although it is natural to think that we would listen better by focusing solely on the other person, much distraction comes from our own thinking -- the train of thoughts that runs continuously, generating judgments, beliefs and even fantasies, all the while removing us from what is actually happening. By directing part of our attention to our own sensations, we can train ourselves to stay present. Doing so also helps us avoid the often reflexive tendency to analyze the other person's appearance and mannerisms, which again serves only to distract us from the truth. Rather, we are receiving our child as a soul - a fully human presence in our midst. The goal of deep listening is to pay attention to that.

Deep listening is not something we need to do every time we communicate with our children, but being with them in this way on a regular basis can deepen our connection in a way that fosters both mutual and soul-to-soul recognition, and teaches them to see themselves in the way we see them – as who they truly are.

Wanting - A Natural Impulse

The presence of empathy allows children to relax – it allows them to feel whatever they feel, and to desire whatever they desire, without judgment, and without limitation. From a very young age, children know what they want and tend to ask for it freely. How we respond to this expression of wanting throughout their lives has an impact on their life experience and their relationships. We teach them whether or not it is okay to want things, especially things that are hard to get.

I remember, as a young child, seeing a commercial for a cool toy and in the spirit of desire, asking my father if I could have it. He would characteristically respond immediately with, "Yes." [pause for effect] "if you have the money for it", which created a roller-coaster of emotions in me which ended with the conclusion that I really will never get that toy. I think, in retrospect, that he was trying to teach me a lesson about the fact that things cost money, and that I must have money in order to buy them.

Such a teaching seems practical and useful in terms of learning about money and self-reliance, but we want to be careful that we do not unknowingly convey the message that it is not okay to *want*. I often find myself speaking to my own children in a way that conveys this message, and I am left once again with the role of practicing restorative communication with my child, reminding them very directly that wanting is a wonderful thing and it is always okay to want what we want – that we can often feel great joy by wanting.

We can also discover the deeper source of that joy if we ask them, "What will having that thing do for you?" We move from what the head thinks it wants to what the heart wants. If their answer is, "It will be fun.", then we can talk about wanting to have fun, which is centered in the heart. We do not have to buy them everything they *say* they want in order to give them what they *truly* want. Fulfilling a temporary wish will create happy feelings, but only until the next commercial or shiny thing comes along. Touching into the source of their happiness, which lies in their heart, teaches them how to be happy even when they have nothing.

Self-Image and Empathy

One of the core teachings in virtually all major spiritual traditions, as well as among the principal psychological paradigms, is that what we take ourselves to be and what we are truly are not the same thing. The process of development is largely considered to be the process of personality development, yet the personality is what we take ourselves to be.

The question that begs to be asked -- its tongue drooling and tail wagging -- is how do we reconcile the genuine importance of the healthy development of personality and self-image with the deep spiritual and psychological truth that we are not, in essence, these things? Why develop a personality and self-image in the first place, and how do we overcome this conundrum within the context of parenting practices?

Our children will learn to see themselves how we see them, at least partially, so the more we can reflect back their essential natures to them, the less disconnected from their natures they will be. Regardless of our good practices and truthful theories, however, children will necessarily remain largely independent in choosing the self-images with which they identify. One child might see a basketball player and be immediately inspired to emulate and take on the identity of that person, even pretending to be them. It won't be long before they are saying, "I am a basketball player." Another child might see Gandhi or Mother Theresa and say, "I am a peacemaker."

Yet our children are also ready – even *eager* – to hear us tell them what they are: "You are so smart", "You are so stubborn", "You are so artistic", etc. -- and they will identify with any such image until the world either reinforces that image for them or convincingly reminds them that their parents simply don't know what they're talking about. I once heard a comedian say that when she grew up, the world failed convincingly to reinforce the princess image that her father had instilled.

I was once in a workshop where the group was told to write down the ten most important self-identifications that each person maintained (e.g., I am a husband, I am a parent, I am a boss, I am a friend, etc.), each on a separate piece of paper, and to order them in importance from one to ten. We were then told to hold up each statement, separately and counting backwards from number ten, all the while sensing each statement into our identities, then crumpling it up and throwing it away. By the time I had counted back to number one, which in my case was "I am a father", I was struck deeply both by a recognition of how important some of the identifications were to me and the simultaneous sense of the liberation that came with the dis-identification from those self-pronouncements.

Although I may be a husband, father, surveyor, mediator, writer, guitar player, and who knows what else, at a much more fundamental level, I am none of those things. I took on those identities as I matured in the world, partly as a conscious choice and partly as the result of unconscious adaptive responses to the situations in which I found myself. Fundamentally, however, well underneath those choices and adaptations, is a truer "me", a truer ground of my own essential being.

PRACTICE: What triggers you?

This practice is meant to provide a doorway into our triggers and to promote personal awareness of both how they arise and how we tend to respond to them. You can do this with a partner, where one person poses the questions below and the other responds in the moment with whatever comes up for them. In this scenario, the person asking the questions does not give feedback or otherwise respond in any way to the sharing by the other person. You can also do this alone by finding a quiet space and writing out and reflecting upon your responses. The questions are as follows:

What triggers you?

How do you know when you are triggered?

What are the physical sensations?

What are the thoughts that come to you when you are triggered?

How do you recover from being triggered?

"Compassion automatically invites you to relate with people because you no longer regard people as a drain on your energy."
Chogyam Trungpa

Chapter 4

PATIENCE

Imagine peace amidst chaos. We often think of peace and chaos as being mutually exclusive, but if we examine our experiences more closely, we will see that there is more happening than we initially perceive. The chaos of a household or car, with human beings from the same family in it, is an experience that we are all familiar with. Behind and underneath the kaleidoscopic chaos, however, lies a state of peace. Not only is peace always present and accessible, it is a primordial, foundational state of our lives. We must simply develop a relationship with it to where we can readily see order in the disorder.

Patience, as it is used here, represents mental resilience and a capacity to recognize our own personality structures as they present themselves in the present, and with that awareness to identify not with those structures but with the underlying, eternal source of love and basic trust upon which our souls depend. We find upon close examination of these structures that, in contrast to the more boundless qualities, they are both unstable and transient in their nature.

The Transient Nature of Resentment[21]

Resentment is transient, and similar in its transiency to the nature of suffering, the nature of ego, and the nature of chaos we so often encounter. This idea is for me the most important in Restorative Parenting, because it can be so liberating when one sees it clearly. Thoughts, emotions, events, and people come in and go out of our awareness. It all comes and goes, and the question is what's left? What is it that truly remains in the midst of all of this coming and going?

The background against which all phenomena arise is open, clear and limitless. It is this spacious field that provides our reference point – our source of not-knowing that provides refuge from the discursive pull of transient emotions that would otherwise drag us into our graves.

The Birth of Resentment

Resentment comes and goes, but from where does it initially arise? Since the underlying and constant backdrop of our experience is present both before the resentment arises and after its demise, it stands to reason that it must also be the ground from which it springs. A thought is hatched from that spacious infinite ground and within a fraction of a second, resentment is initiated with the reactionary unconscious release of one thought, coupled with the emotional response that accompanies it, which is quickly followed by a train of thoughts rolling down a track, with each new thought stoking the engine again and again.

Distracted by this fast, noisy locomotive, we neglect the vast frontier of mountains, rivers, clouds and awe-inspiring beauty -- the very setting that could otherwise provide peace of mind. We are left with a setting which is constant, vast and spacious, yet also with temporary thoughts and resentments that distract us from its beauty. It is these numerous and continuous distractions that keep us from recognizing the true eternal landscape of our experience.

The next important question is *why* does the resentment arise? An underlying assumption of all psychological activity is that it must serve some purpose. This is where the convergence of psychology, esoteric philosophy, and spiritual work occurs. There is the ground of our being that supports the whole human life experience, and there is the drama of the experience playing itself out on that ground.

All the while, there remains a natural potential to expose and remove the veil that obscures our perspective. This, in my view, is the reason and meaning for the presence of resentment and other conflicting emotions. It represents the potential for perceptual clarity that challenges us to look deeply enough at our chaotic and often bizarrely infantile emotions in order to see through resentment's deception, and expand our perspective until we can hold it without reacting.

Resentment comes and goes, and often feeds on itself over time, gradually bolstered and supported by new information. The problem is that upon the initial leap toward resentment, such new information can be tainted by a bias drawn from the activation of core wounds and values. This is why it helps us to increase our awareness of how we respond physically and emotionally to interpersonal stimuli, and work to come back to a state of not-knowing, as discussed in more detail later in this chapter. We have to take personal responsibility for our levels of awareness, and we do so by always being willing to not know.

The Ground of Resentment

Everything arises out of the ground. Ego, projection and resentment all arise out of one's Essence, which can be interpreted as True Nature, Ground of Being, Spirit and a number of other terms related to the essential quality of Beingness. I choose to use the term Essence here because is connotes to me a concept that is fairly free from baggage. Everything, including ego, arises out of Essence and even ego therefore represents Essence – it may be a narrow, ignorant form of Essence, but it is Essence nevertheless, even if merely in a symbolic or representative form[22].

Everything arises in our awareness and then passes from it. Suffering and fear come from wanting to hold some things in our awareness and to keep other things out of it, or from simply not paying attention to what is arising. Freedom from suffering and fear comes from allowing what is in our awareness to remain there without judgment, assumption or preconception.

Through the development of *equanimity*, we can honestly assess the motives of others and respond accordingly, with compassion and understanding. This is a primordial capacity among human beings – one that speaks deeply to our incredible adaptability. And we can enhance our natural and instinctual capacity for equanimity by training our conscious mind through practices that enhance concentration and awareness.

The foundational components of patience are nurtured and strengthened through practice.

Basic Dignity

Meditation is, for me, a chance to reconnect with the inherent basic dignity that we were all born with and retain throughout our lives. Yet modern culture does not, by and large, reflect our basic dignity back to us. Rather it prefers to point out our shortcomings and failures.

This tendency for our environment to highlight our imperfections can be detrimental to our sense of self-worth, creating an internal thought-loop that reinforces those negative messages over and over again, regardless of any resistance we may muster. This internalized oppression is a particularly well-documented phenomenon among persecuted and oppressed peoples.

The value in recognizing this inconvenient truth is that as we explore the inner workings of this messaging system, we realize more and more how any self-image, whether it appears to be attractive or not, is false. It is simply a voice in our head. The truth of our being is found instead in the basic dignity that we encounter when we call out the voices for what they are – namely, mere thinking.

In short, one of the most important things to remember about meditation and self-realization is that *we are not our thoughts*. We are, every one of us, in our true natures, fundamentally dignified people who have valuable gifts to offer the world. Every time we sit down to meditate, we connect directly with this aspect of our selves – this *basic sanity* – this *basic goodness* – and override the loss of clarity so often imposed by our thoughts.

As we connect with and identify more and more with our own and others' basic dignity, starting from that place as we encounter the world, we find, inevitably and miraculously, that our worlds reflect our basic dignity back to us. We also find that this basic dignity becomes less obscured in the real world, allowing us to reflect it back to our children and vice-versa.

In a PBS special on brain plasticity[23], a study was conducted on people with obsessive-compulsive disorder in which the subjects were instructed that upon encountering obsessive thoughts or impulses to engage in compulsive behaviors (e.g., repeatedly checking that the stove is turned off), they should resist with statements such as "It's just my thoughts telling me this" and "It's not true". The approach showed significant success, with subjects who employed the technique (changing how they related to their thoughts) exhibiting just as much improvement as those who took medications.

Likewise in meditation, we too can recognize that our thoughts are just our thoughts: We label them as "thinking" and come back to our breath[24]. This practice both reveals our basic dignity and supports physiological changes in our brains, promoting clarity and meaningful contact with others in our environments.

This is not to suggest that thinking itself is somehow inherently negative. Thoughts are not the enemy -- on the contrary, they can be very useful when guided by intention. The goal is to avoid allowing thoughts to distract us from reality by not accepting the false "intelligence" they so often bring. We need not ignore or deny thoughts – rather, we observe them as the distractions they are, yet refuse to be captured by or identify with them.

The Present Moment

The present moment is all we need, and it is all we have. The clear and profound wonder of spiritual realization, as achieved through meditative awareness, is that even if we sometimes feel guilty for wasting our time with television and other generally useless pursuits, we needn't be overly worried because in truth we have "missed" absolutely nothing. It is never too late because the openness that we taste in the present moment never dissipates and never ceases to be available.

We never lose potential for ultimate awareness and cosmic consciousness – rather, pure bliss is an integral part of our makeup and it is found only in the present moment. The fact that we never made a million dollars or became famous doing what we love has no effect on our capacity for happiness. In the present moment, we will find, that we have all we need, and that our value is within.

Of course we must begin to work with the true conditions of our lives when we become aware of them in order to bring balance and synchronicity to our existences, but this is all relative in light of the simplicity and workability of the present moment – the right now. In our lives and in our relationships with our children, there is no such thing as too late. We can always work with what is right in front of us, regardless of how difficult it may seem.

The essence of patience then is simply to: 1) pay attention; 2) let what is in our awareness pass, particularly if it triggers us, before we act; and 3) act with intelligent compassion as opposed to mindless compassion. Our intention is to be present, productive, sober, loving and attentive.

Each expression from our children deserves our awareness as parents. No response is necessary -- only awareness. Fathers especially tend to get stuck with the instinct that they must do something about the expression when in truth it is not necessary to DO anything but rather simply be aware and empathize with the expression.

Of course it is sometimes necessary to act, be it under a protective impulse or as a supportive and healing impulse. Skillful action, however, arises only out of awareness, so awareness, in the present moment, must always precede action.

Three Aspects of Mindfulness

At the core of our capacity to parent in a way that honors our integrity and minimizes harm is the ability to be mindful. By mindful, I mean the opposite of mindless – a state in which we are unaware of our surroundings and the impact of our words and actions. Although this mindful state ties into the notions of the adult state, awareness, and presence as discussed previously, there are further more subtle aspects to consider as well.

First, mindfulness is founded in the faculty of *restfulness*. When we are mindful, our minds must be at rest, not jumping from thought to thought with each passing whim distracting our attention. No thoughts are allowed to take hold of us – we simply witness our thoughts as they come and go. We rely on our ability to let go of stimuli and become restful in both body and consciousness as the stimuli present themselves in our present experience.

Second, mindfulness is grounded in an expression of *gentleness*. The violence that emerges from unconscious influences may be present, but it will not be in charge. It is not allowed to act because the responsible, truly empowered adult is ultimately in charge. The gentleness that we extend to our kids is also extended to ourselves. We are aware of the influences on our present state and we shift them with empathy and gentleness.

A third aspect of mindfulness is *precision*, which is notable for its protective quality. When we are practicing mindfulness, especially in the midst of chaos, we can often encounter difficulty in sustaining a mindful state of consciousness. In response, we emphasize precision in our approach, adopting our practice when we have a few minutes of quiet privacy. We practice our unwavering attention to our present states of mind and body. We consistently come back to the spaciousness of the reality that pervades our existence, underneath the surface mental activity, and with the knowledge that mindfulness is available to us even in times of crisis.

We are conscious of our bodies and what they are telling us in terms of health, fatigue, and aliveness. We are attentive to our breathing and the rhythm it assumes as it delivers oxygen to our brain and lungs. We witness our thoughts, and the emotions that accompany them, and we are tuned into the auditory and visual nature of our environment. This may sound like some sort of "Jedi" approach – and indeed in many ways, it is. In truth, the practices that make a great mythical cosmic warrior are the same ones that make a great parent.

The Seven Arts of Zen Parenting

1. Bodhisattva Parent

The bodhisattva represents an enlightened being who, rather than escaping the perpetual re-birth cycle and remaining in a state of perpetual Buddhahood, chooses instead to humble himself of herself and return to the human form with the mission to relieve the suffering of other beings.

In similar fashion, it can be said that there is no responsibility more humbling than that of a parent. From the time our children are born we quickly realize that our lives are no longer our own (if they ever were...) and that we now serve a new master and a greater good. If a healthy attachment has developed, we instinctively relinquish self-concern in the interest of our children's safety and health. As our attachment deepens, we recognize that our sacrifice is worthy of our mission and we continue to put aside our own pleasure and convenience to support them in their development.

However, as our children grow and become less dependent, there may be a tendency to lose sight of our original inspiration and to seek reciprocity in terms of need fulfillment. It is a mistake to expect our children to meet our emotional needs. The element of unconditional love that is present at the birth of our child must continually be nurtured and acknowledged.

The mission to take care of our children and to live in the service of their healthy maturation and physical, intellectual, emotional and spiritual growth must be renewed on a daily basis. Our initial intention to serve their needs regardless of the time of day or night, and regardless of their intention or ability to return the favor, is a humble undertaking that lasts a lifetime.

I am not suggesting here that we merely clean up after our children's messes with no expectations and no consequences for behaviors that conflict with our values. To the contrary, the servant mission itself requires a focus on instilling character and responsibility. That said, we must not forget the primacy of simply connecting with our children every day on a personal level. We talk to them, listen to them, maintain eye contact with them, and keep their needs in mind in all cases.

2. Concentration

One of the principle benefits of meditation is that it develops concentration, and one of the most basic and profound practices in meditation is in learning how to follow your breath. The practice of keeping our attention on a single point of focus – in this case, our breathing -- trains the mind to stay with our present experience and relieves us of the habitual tendency to be distracted by the endless stream of repetitive thoughts running through our heads at any given moment.

It is in reflexive and reactionary thoughts, and the emotions that accompany them, that we ultimately disrupt our intentions to parent the way we want to. Parenting is done best when it is done in the present moment, without the influence of preconceived notions or subconscious neuroses inherited from our own childhood experiences. And it is through concentration that we can develop a non-attachment to the discursive thoughts that would threaten our openness to our present experiences, and as such represents possibly the most valuable skill we can have in life as well as parenting.

3. *Loving Kindness*

Metta practice in Buddhism is a practice of wishing well to yourself and all other beings. In this respect, it is very important that we start first with ourselves. For one, we cannot serve our children or anyone else very well if our own needs are not met.

On a more universal scale, we should recognize that we, in our essence, represent all beings. Indeed, the interdependence of all aspects of our own existence with that of all beings is a fundamental part of connecting to truth itself, and some suggest that the very illusion of separateness is the source of all of our suffering in the first place. Of course, on a more routine basis, we do mostly experience ourselves as separate, and that's what makes it so important to approach any persistent sense of separate existence in a caring, loving and forgiving way.

We may endeavor to emanate only positive caring intentions, and will that these intentions radiate out to all. In doing so, we start with ourselves in order to empathize with the wounded aspects of our own psyches, in order to be able to give to others from a place of wholeness. In all of us there remains a vulnerable and wounded child who seeks safety and unconditional love.

Luckily, if we develop an awareness of him or her, we are in a position to provide to our children the deep-seeded sense of safety and acceptance that they too long for. They, after all, are confronted and confounded in the present by their own vulnerabilities. It is in our hands to either unknowingly facilitate the repression of these vulnerabilities, or to help them learn to harness these challenges as some of the most powerful sources of intelligence they will ever know.

As we practice self-empathy and feel the benefits of it personally, we can radiate that skill and quality to those we care most about, to those for whom we have neutral feelings, and even to those with whom we have conflict or difficulty. This further widening of our scope of care and concern can generate an even more supportive context in which our children can thrive with a clear and purposeful moral compass.

4. Egolessness

As one of the Buddha's three marks of existence, egolessness represents the essence of our primordial being, prior to and independent of ego. Ego here represents our self-image – how we see ourselves and how the world sees us, and is tied to our accomplishments, failures, jobs, and social and cultural roles.

But we also have another self, a true self, that has been with us through life and is independent of those things – and is likewise independent of our thoughts, emotions, judgments and dreams. This True Self is accessible to us and we can develop a consciousness that is not only aware of this self, but also operates from it.

Our roles as parents and adults are just that – roles that we step into in order to fulfill specific functions in society and in our relationships. These functions and roles are not without value. Indeed, they serve an important purpose in our efforts to organize our worlds in ways that make sense, based on our perspectives.

By developing an awareness of our egolessness, and taking on the parenting role with a sense of both autonomy and engaged attachment, we can, like master actors, facilitate a more objective perspective and stop tying our identities and self-images to either the success of our children or their expressions and behaviors.

We learn not to take things personally. We are no longer tied to the outcome of any situation. Only when we cease being attached to outcomes will we be able to connect with our children in the moment. They are always trying to express unmet needs, and when those expressions are seemingly offensive or overly personal, we can become blind to the truth behind them. The less we take their expressions personally, the more clearly we will hear them.

5. *Equanimity*

Even after we train ourselves in concentration, we can continue to have random thoughts and then tend to make judgments about those thoughts as to whether they are good or bad.

Developing the quality of equanimity is a process of freeing ourselves completely from notions of blame, justification, or the need to be right. There is a complete acceptance of everything as it is and for what it is – with no such thing as good or bad. Rather, there is simply something arising in our awareness and it has attributes that define it. It may be one child screaming for you to get them a glass of milk or another child telling you that you look nice. In either case, we don't put extra judgments on the thing that is happening – where something requires a response, we simply respond in the most skillful way possible.

Equanimity also represents an *absolute* understanding of reality or what might be seen as the background against which all *relative* phenomena occur.

For us to be equanimous as parents means to be in touch with the most essential aspects of ourselves -- the source of our potential understanding and wisdom.

Equanimity also means to be in touch with our own mortality and the transient nature of our existence. We are here in this body for now, but we soon will not be. How will we spend this time we have? Will we spend it judging and blaming and complaining of our troubles or will we represent our inherent essence and dignity, and meet those in our lives always recognizing theirs, regardless of the circumstances?

6. "Start Where You Are"

Buddhist teacher and author Pema Chodron wrote a book with this title, one that speaks directly to our ability to accept things as they are. We often wish that our lives were as we envision them in daydreams, and become impatient and irritable in the midst of the real thing playing itself out.

We wish we were the greatest parents possible, the most successful in our careers, and most happy in our relationships. But all of us reside at some point along a continuum of growth in all of those capacities, and the more willing we are to embrace where we are and get to work from that place, the more content and productive we will be.

7. *Koan Practice*

Koan practice in Zen is a way to develop an enlightened perspective through the use of obscure ancient dialogues documented by Zen masters. The student is intended to reflect on the dialogue and present his or her understanding to the teacher. The infinite value of koans in this context is that they do not have a single answer.

Although there are certain understandings that contribute to the solving of a koan, the key to getting at its heart is to see it working in one's own life, with one's own situation, as it is right now. The trick to employing the wisdom of Zen, and all essential truth, in our lives is just that – taking ultimate eternal truths and making them a force in daily life by applying them to our situations. As someone who has attended many Catholic masses, I have encountered certain priests who can do this in their homilies as adeptly as Zen Masters, yet others who would simply put you to sleep. The point is that unless we can bring spiritual teachings into our own situations, both painful and joyful, they are not of much use to us. The truly enlightened teachers, regardless of their affiliations, know this.

The Three Tenets of Peacemaking

The three tenets of the Zen Peacemaker Order, founded by Roshi Bernie Glassman[25], are: not knowing, bearing witness, and loving action. To say that parents are peacemakers by occupation is to speak to an inherent and profound truth about our roles and work. Indeed, to be committed to any relationship is to be engaged in a peacemaking mission that requires the highest level of consciousness available at any given time. Our peacemaking activities, within the home, extend to all of the relationships, among all of the family members, all of the time. And, as with the practice of loving kindness, peacemaking starts with ourselves.

We must practice making peace with our own conflicts -- inner and outer -- conscious and unconscious. We can learn to tame conflicting thoughts and emotions in the midst of challenging circumstances, and thus raise ourselves up from the otherwise low levels of consciousness that accompany those challenges.

1. Not-Knowing

We start by first taking a position of "not-knowing," actively embracing a philosophy of not knowing the answer, the future, or the particulars of a situation. When we believe we know someone, we preconceive how they will present themselves to us, what they will say, what they will look like, as well as their talents and usefulness regarding certain tasks.

This is no way to be in relationship. By knowing, we separate the situation or the person from ourselves and this is not what we desire in relationships. Instead, what we desire is intimacy and connection, and these will not come if we approach the relationship with thinking we know everything.

You can see this by looking at a new romantic relationship – at first, two people are falling in love and embracing in this great sea of not-knowing, yet once they believe they have learned everything about the other person, the relationship can become habitual and lacking in spontaneity.

The very act of knowing ironically makes something unknowable in its present form. So you can see how important it is for a peacemaker to embrace this not-knowing philosophy, for it is in not-knowing that the truth reveals itself. By taking a not-knowing position, we resist the urge to react to a situation in a way that is hurtful rather than helpful. Instead, we take the time necessary to see things clearly as they are before we act.

Socrates is regarded by many as the greatest Western philosopher of all time, and he reportedly spoke of the value of ignorance in his approach to philosophical problems. He was not speaking of ignorance in the sense of ignoring the truth, but rather in the sense of ignoring the habitual thoughts that initially arise in the face of the problems. He was interested in getting at the insights that arise after shooing away preconceptions – to the deeper and more eternal truth.

2. Bearing Witness

Once we have adopted an approach of not-knowing, we are in a position to bear witness to things, people and situations as they actually are, in the present moment. We view things with fresh eyes, unencumbered by prejudice and obscuration. We see clearly not only the thing, but also how our own thoughts and feelings arise in response to it.

With our children, we open ourselves to sense into their feelings and needs, as well as our own, and come gradually to know what is required in the situation. It is when we are in this most humble and natural state of observation that we experience the deepest sense of connection with our kids, and the joy that arises is unmistakable.

Think of when your child was an infant and you held them and looked into their eyes with no fixed ideas about who they were or what to expect from them. Think of the profound love that is present in that simple connection, a love that inspires a perfectly appropriate response to their needs, without words, without instruction, without knowing – but simply in being present with such an intimate connection.

3. Loving Action

I have heard it said and seen it written that parents have all the tools they need to parent well and simply must follow their natural parenting instincts. The first part of this sounds reasonable to me, but the thought of relying on instinct is perhaps less so. Instincts are derived from our so-called reptilian brains and by and large merely direct our responses toward the singular goal of survival.

The innate natural tools that we possess are few – we may have the skills necessary to keep a child alive to adulthood, but the development of a meaningful, lifelong relationship takes practice and work. We must develop patience and the discriminating insight that is required to model and teach both emotional intelligence and needs intelligence.

Just doing what our fathers and mothers did will not honor their desires and intentions for us to excel beyond and evolve the family tree. We have a purpose to evolve the species as well, and that evolution comes in the form of an increased capacity to love and show genuine compassion toward each other.

The love, compassion and skillful means that emerge from this evolved consciousness arise as the natural consequence of practicing the first two tenets of not-knowing and bearing witness. Authentic and effective loving action arises naturally out of paying close attention after checking our assumptions.

PRACTICE: Meditation

Meditation is a time-honored technique for cultivating mindfulness. Every major spiritual tradition includes some form (or forms) of meditation practice, and people all over the world practice meditation as part of a lifestyle aimed simply at increasing their sense of well-being. Through meditation, the obstacles to patience become more visible and the inherent qualities of patience become more accessible. In my experience, a true and meaningful realization of pure patience is rare if not impossible without regular meditation practice.

Benefits of Meditation

Brain: As with all mindfulness practices, meditation strengthens the communication of the pre-frontal cortex (the wisdom center of the brain) with other areas of the brain, improving overall brain functionality.

Stress: Chronic stress is one of the most damaging factors for the brain and body. Meditation reduces stress by creating new neural pathways between the brain's left and right hemispheres, balancing the two.

Creativity: Meditation promotes an optimal mental environment for creativity.

Happiness: Meditation has been shown to increase the level of reported happiness.

Health: Many studies have shown significant health benefits from meditation, including reduced incidence of heart disease. It has been found to be a key lifestyle factor in patients who have shown dramatic recovery from life-threatening diseases.

Concentration: Meditation practice develops our capacity for concentration, which significantly impacts our ability to tame the ever-thinking mind. We can recapture the time we spend meditating because it gives us the capacity to do more in less time.

Equanimity: By clearing the cloudiness of the mind, and awakening wisdom, we are able to broaden our perspectives, reducing the excesses of judgment in our points of view.

Reactivity: One of the additional effects of calming the mind and taming our thoughts is that we become less reactive. We can look at our painful emotions without blaming others, slowing down our reactive tendencies.

Energy: By relaxing the mind and limbic system, we find that we have access to abundant physical and mental energy.

Empathy: Meditation increases blood flow to the area of the brain that mediates empathy, social awareness, intuition, compassion, and the ability to regulate emotions.

Basic Meditation Instruction

Take a comfortable sitting posture. Sitting cross-legged on a meditation cushion is great but a chair works just fine as well. Bring awareness to your posture. A straight but not tensed spine brings dignity and a better result to your practice. A relaxed face and mouth helps the rest of the body feel relaxed. Sit in such a way that you are comfortable and present. Rest your palms on your thighs. If you are in a chair, place both feet flat on the floor. Then begin to follow your breath.

Put your full awareness into following your breath - the in-breath and the out-breath. When thoughts arise – which they will – don't get caught up and carried away by them. Don't evaluate the thoughts or judge yourself for being distracted. Just say silently and gently to yourself "thinking" and bring your awareness back to your breath.

Because generating thoughts is the mind's default activity, the process of noticing thoughts and coming back to the breath is repeated over and over. The moment in which you notice that you are distracted is actually very potent, so rather than perceiving yourself as a failure at that moment, you have actually found the key to your liberation from suffering.

Do this for 20 minutes per day, every day for a month, and see what you notice. Timing the meditation helps to remove any tendency to play games with yourself about when to end the session. Of course there is no set rule about how long to meditate -- 5 minutes per day is better than nothing, and an hour per day may just alleviate all of life's conflicts and difficulties.

The benefits of meditation come with the fierce commitment to truth and self-understanding inherent in the act of coming back to the breath, again and again – a commitment to interrupt the habit of getting lost in every thought and fantasy.

In making such a commitment, you will gradually develop more control of your mind. The ability to be less reactive to every automatic impulse is strengthened. Meditation practice also increases the sense of well-being and your ability to manage conflict in your relationships. The mind feels more sane and life becomes more workable.

*"It is easy to dodge our responsibilities, but we cannot dodge
the consequences of dodging our responsibilities."*
Josiah Charles Stamp

Chapter 5

ADULTHOOD

There is no such thing as a dysfunctional family, only dysfunctional parents. One of the mantras of Mahayana Buddhism is to "Drive all blames into one." The point is not to create a cycle of self-blame, where everything is the parents' fault, but rather to remind ourselves that the source of our adult capacity to be in meaningful and empowered relationship with our world is within us. The power is with us if choose to accept it. As soon as we find ourselves pointing fingers, we start to see our competence and insight recede into the ashes of the fire of our resentment. The way to regain our virtue, our dignity, and our natural intelligence is to simply accept responsibility.

Fully Empowered Adult Perspective

A *fully empowered adult perspective*[26] is a state of consciousness distinguished by characteristics grounded in *responsibility,* and is attained through the fundamental principles of *restorative practice.* We lecture our children on how they must learn to take responsibility and we are sometimes baffled by their inability or downright refusal to do so. Yet how often do we contemplate our own capacity to take responsibility for the harms we cause in our daily lives?

Are we taking responsibility for our own passivity when we are called to be proactive, or conversely, for our rigidity when the situation calls for flexibility and compassion? How are we, as adults, modeling adulthood and responsibility for our children and others who look to us for leadership? What are the characteristics of the adult perspective? What are the obstacles and habitual tendencies that sabotage a truly adult mindset? And how do we shift into a fully empowered adult perspective in the face of challenging circumstances?

The fully empowered adult perspective exists when we take personal responsibility in the present moment and give priority to relationships by deciding that they are more important than being "right." When our actions have contributed to suffering in any way, including self-harm, we hold ourselves accountable by the steps we take to repair the harm and to heal the sense of alienation that occurs within the relationship and toward the community at large.

Maintaining an awareness of when we are thinking and acting in ways that undermine the adult perspective is the key to accessing it in the first place. We know that we are not in our fully adult state when one or more of the following defense mechanisms are present: Needing to be right, resentment, justification, and blame.

Being right is a defensive strategy by which we temporarily protect our notions of self and dignity in relation to the outside world. Ironically, this impulse does not contribute to our sense of confidence, security or self-worth, nor does it create peace or promote conflict resolution. A teacher of mine once said, "Everything is true, in a particular context – broaden the context and it ceases to be true." So, we work to broaden the context – not to make ourselves wrong, but to discover what is right in other perspectives.

Resentment distinguishes itself by the perception that we have been harmed by the actions of another, and when we succumb to this mindset we take on the role of victim and simultaneously relinquish our capacity for agency as to the outcome of the situation. In other words, we project our own sense of deficiency onto someone else, thereby childishly relieving ourselves of responsibility, and unfortunately, consciousness and truth. Author Malachy McCourt once said that resentment is like taking poison and waiting for the other person to die.

Justification arises in the creation of a false reality to match our own perspective rather than adapting our viewpoint to match the truth of the situation. This is where our inner lawyer comes in. With all due respect to lawyers, the sole ambition of this perspective is to get us off the hook. Sadly, in relationships, no one wins when we give ourselves a pass, especially us.

Blaming is a way of protecting the self from the vulnerability inherently raised by a difficult situation – we feel exposed and naturally want to cover up. It results in the isolation and alienation of both parties. The lure of blame and the easy availability of someone else to blame becomes all too attractive: This failure simply has to be someone's fault. There may also be a tendency to self-blame, and in this case we must distinguish the impulse to blame ourselves as a way of self-punishing from the adult act of taking responsibility in a way that restores our sense of confidence and capacity. The former is almost invariably destructive, whereas the latter is truly empowering from an adult perspective.

At the moment we observe ourselves in any one of the four states above, it is important to note that we have, in that observation taken the most important step toward an empowered adult state. As the psychotherapist and founder of gestalt therapy, Fritz Perls, observed, "awareness in and of itself is curative." As soon as we become aware of our destructive tendencies, in the present moment, we have begun to dis-identify from them, which in turn gives us the strength to take our power back from their negative effects.

By making our habits (positive or negative) conscious -- and naming them explicitly -- we see them for what they are. They are psychological constructs, created when we were children as defense mechanisms against a complex and often scary world. Yet they are mechanisms that not only are no longer needed for protection, they also degrade our capacities to approach the world in real and meaningful ways.

Once we are aware of our defense mechanisms and their effects, we become more open to seeing where we can take responsibility and shift our concern to our relationships. By shifting into a truly empowered adult perspective, we reclaim our power by taking responsibility for our lives as they are. As the Buddhist meditation master Chogyam Trungpa said so disarmingly, "The more we give our best, the more we are able to receive other people's worst. Isn't that great?"

Responsibility Equals Empowerment

The Drama Triangle and the unconscious use of power. The so-called "Drama Triangle" is a tool historically employed in transactional analysis, and is in wide use today in psychology, business, and human-potential workshops. It was first described by Stephen Karpman in 1968, and postulates three roles -- victim, persecutor, and rescuer -- which we unconsciously assume as defensive strategies in conflict situations. We jump into the triangle instinctively both when we are triggered and when we are simply communicating from a mindless place. The ensuing consequences can be catastrophic from a relationship standpoint.

What makes good drama? In the movies, on television, and in our lives, the roles of victim, persecutor and rescuer help fuel the dramatic plot line brought on by conflict. In real life, the difference from fiction is that we suffer the consequences of this drama far more directly by exacerbating already dysfunctional aspects of our relationships.

It is easy to see how this dynamic can play out in our interactions with our kids. We feel victimized by our children when they leave their wet towels on the hallway floor, their wrappers and other garbage in a trail through the house, or their dirty dishes virtually everywhere, as well as by their refusals to take responsibility for their existence or show respect to their elders.

The feeling of victimization can easily transform us into a persecutor where we are condemning our kids for being inconsiderate and disrespectful. The second parent is then poised to enter as the child's rescuer under a "house divided" scenario, thus filling out the third point in the drama triangle and creating a destructive dynamic between the parents.

Why do we so readily turn to the drama triangle? We take on these roles because they give us power in the relationships in question. We may either exercise power over others by persecuting or rescuing them, or we may exercise power from the place of victimhood by claiming that we are the "good ones."

All of these positions of power fulfill a need for us to be in control of ourselves, our relationships, and our destinies in the face of chaos and conflict. Chaos and conflict are scary and the insecurity that comes from unexpected circumstances causes us to react under a strong urge for control and predictability. We instinctively cling to forms of control and power that come naturally and are readily available, adopting roles that allow us to avoid taking responsibility or even reflecting on our reactive and emotional states of heart and mind.

Awareness is curative. Just as when we notice ourselves experiencing blame, resentment, justification or the need to be right, noticing which role we tend to play on the triangle can give us the power to change the dynamic. We need to notice not only which of the four unempowered defense mechanisms we are adopting but also which of the three roles of the triangle we happen to be coming from in the moment. Where do these dysfunctional impulses come from? Why do we tend to choose this particular role in this situation?

Notably, the positions on the triangle can be highly fluid and dynamic. I will often embody all three roles within the period of a minute when engaged in a difficult discussion with my wife or my kids. Yet what we find if we inquire fully into our tendencies regarding these roles is that they do not actually give us power. Rather, they tend only to further disrupt our relationships and alienate us from those we want to be in relationship with.

True Power. When we are stuck on the drama triangle, we are not adopting a fully empowered adult perspective. We can get off the triangle and into our adult perspectives by taking responsibility and making our relationships the priority, in the present moment. Our true source of power comes from taking responsibility for our lives as they are. The process of getting off of the triangle -- of taking responsibility, staying present and giving our relationships priority over the need to be right -- begins again under the approach of "not–knowing" as discussed more fully in the previous chapter. We must develop the capacity to tolerate the insecurity and stress that can arise in the face of not reacting, and rather check in with our experience without the need to act, even where we might otherwise feel compelled to do so.

We have learned how checking in with our physical sensations can inform us in deeply profound ways, as well as how self-empathy is the key to the practice of empathy for others. Still, none of these practices or qualities can truly kick in if we don't allow ourselves to feel that first few seconds (or minutes) of the irritation and discomfort that comes with not knowing. We must allow our senses to resolve the emotional and amygdala-driven reactions that are otherwise hard-wired into our pasts, presents and futures, and to do so we must first notice and inquire.

Inquiry Practice

Often, when we look closely at our experience, we find a degree of pain, fear or withdrawal. The best attitude in the context of Inquiry[27] is to be open to these feelings and to explore them. When we allow our feelings to simply remain within our experience without trying to reject, fix or control them, we eventually open up. And when we open up, we reveal our deeper nature, or essence.

Thus, we see that these issues should not be viewed as obstacles to living fully and freely, but rather as gateways to a full and free life. When we reject or try to fix these issues, we block our freedom, richness, intimacy and aliveness. When we open to whatever is happening with attention, curiosity, openness, compassion, courage and sincerity, they lead us deeper and open us more to life.

As such, the inquiry practice reveals one of the most fundamental and important understandings of restorative parenting. All of our experiences, no matter how wonderful or difficult, can lead us deeper, heal us, and bring us closer to our full potential and deepest nature.

As adults, we can and should allow ourselves to have feelings of hatred, anger, resentment, loneliness and fear. Although we may encounter inner messages that tell us it's not okay to feel these things, we must realize that these messages come from our past, from our youth, and from prior wounds, and we can now give ourselves permission to just feel whatever it is we are feeling.

In doing so, we give ourselves the key to our own salvation, and we take adult responsibility for our feelings. When we allow ourselves to feel the anger and hatred, we own the feelings and begin to reduce our tendency to project them onto others, which is the deeper fear for most of us, namely, that we will harm others by lashing out. By feeling fully, we don't have to expel our feelings outward in destructive ways.

When we learn to do this, we likewise learn to accept the feelings our children are experiencing, and can help them feel okay with their emotions rather than projecting our own internal judgments onto them. We can show our children how all of their emotions – both positive and negative -- are normal, helpful, and can point to something essential within their natures.

PRACTICE: 5-Step Inquiry

Not-Knowing, Sensing, Needs, Space, and Essence

Inquiry is an ancient and open-ended concept. Socrates imparted a detailed process of inquiry that involved open-ended questions within internal and external dialogues aimed solely at discovering the truth. Author and spiritual teacher A.H. Almaas[28] further investigated the practice of inquiry, bringing it to the highest form of self-awareness practice available to those ready to do the work.

Inquiry practice as defined here is a simple summary of my own experience. I have defined this basic structure as a way of working with my experience in an intentional way, although a more pure inquiry would be perhaps more open-ended and without direction towards specific experiences or insights.

The inquiry practice below follows the thread of knowing where it leads, building on and heralding capacities that grow and expand in ever more complex and subtle ways. The practice, however it unfolds, is inspired first and foremost by an unyielding pursuit of the truth, whatever it may be.

Step 1: Not-Knowing – As previously discussed, we cannot know unless we first do not know. No, this is not a paraphrase of a notorious Donald Rumsfeld quote – it is rather simply the most straightforward way I can think to impart the notion. In not-knowing, we find the seeds of mindfulness and equanimity. We make a simple intention to let go of preconceived notions and trust our capacity for discernment as we investigate our experience in the present moment.

Step 2: Sensing – Expanding the presence of mindfulness by paying close and careful attention to the sensations in our bodies helps awaken our physical intelligence, which can often communicate more about our experience than anything else. How is energy moving through your body – in your arms and legs? Is there pressure or pain in your head? What are the sensations in your belly, chest and throat?

Step 3: Needs – The two steps above prepare us to perceive, more fully and without reactivity, the place of deficiency that inspires defensiveness and reactivity. In this step, our purpose is to sense into what's missing. One might observe that his or her life and personality lack certain qualities that, if possessed, would increase happiness and fulfillment. At this point, mindfulness evolves into the awareness and intelligence that come with acknowledging our own desires, which themselves spring from a sense of lacking. Our needs thus recognized then lead us to the sense of vulnerability that comes with the presence of space.

Step 4: Space – As we continue to inquire into our deficiencies, we notice a certain vulnerability arises, which is further accompanied by a sense of spaciousness. This place can feel groundless, as though we have lost our footing and ability to predict what will happen.

In the earlier step of not-knowing, we adopted an intention to let go of expectations about what the truth is. In the present step of the inquiry practice, we let ourselves go to a place of space and mystery – a step that requires faith and trust. It can accompany a fluttering heart, and the uncertainty associated with it can engender fear and an impulse to find our way back to solid ground. But if we stay with it, we will see that it is actually the source of primordial intelligence and the doorway to essence.

Step 5: Essence – With the recognition and acceptance of the true spaciousness inherent in our being, we come to true nature – pure universal emptiness and perfect clarity, out of which arises whatever subtle qualities or capacities that are called for in the moment, which in turn may provide further guidance to deeper inquiry.

To give a mundane example of this process, if I am feeling that I have no energy to work out, even though I had planned to, I am lacking the will to simply begin the workout. Additionally, I am receiving internal messages that say, "I can always do it later". So during my inquiry practice, I will acknowledge my lack of desire, which then translates as a lack of willpower, and I will let go of any internal thoughts or opinions that are present prior to the inquiry. As I navigate the inner space beneath the lack of will and the rationalizations, I might gradually start to feel increasing energy in my legs and arms, and before I know it, I'm putting on my running shorts.

So we initially make an intention to let go of our understanding about what is going on, we sense into our bodies, inquire into what it is that we feel we are missing, open ourselves to the spaciousness inherent within our physical and mental presences, and witness the personal capacities that arise naturally to meet the moment.

The practice: Think of a recent situation where you were either embodying one of the roles in the drama triangle or subject to one of the four dis-empowering defense mechanisms discussed earlier in this chapter. Use the 5-step practice above to inquire into it. Whether the process takes 20 minutes or 5 minutes, try to go though it in a deliberate and step-wise fashion. It will get easier with multiple practice sessions.

"Violence produces only something resembling justice, but it distances people from the possibility of living justly, without violence."
Leo Tolstoy

Chapter 6

RESTORATION

Fights, wounding, pain, trouble, conflict and harmful acts and words are gifts. They are all ways that the family system communicates its needs and issues to those who have a stake in it. Unfortunately, when these things occur, we typically look for a person to blame as the source of the trouble, when in fact the so-called culprit is merely the vehicle for the system's communication.

If we can see the trouble in this way, as an initiatory message, we can find the tools to evolve the family system toward a more functional and flourishing structure of precious and talented individuals. We will not only refrain from killing the messenger, we will restore to our children the tools and knowledge to know their own gifts and the power to employ them for the good of the family and the world.

Restorative practices are fundamental, community-oriented approaches to repair harm to our relationships, restore a sense of safety and respect to our relationships, and deepen our relationships in ways that improve their quality and cohesiveness. In my experience, it has been within this process of recognizing when harm has occurred and seeking a way to repair it that most of the quality growth in the family group has taken place. It is here that we discover the greatest opportunity for growth and transformation as a family.

When my youngest son was 5, he and his friend stole his older brother's Halloween hair color spray, took it to the neighbors' house, and proceeded to paint their trees, sidewalk, and a landscaping boulder. When I found out about this, I first wished it hadn't happened at all. I also wished that my wife had been home to deal with it, and even thought about letting it go until she came home. But instead, I decided to start from where I was.

After working through my initial exasperation and frustration, I explained to my son, who was already feeling very ashamed, that he was not a "bad" person for doing this, but that what he and his friend did had damaged our neighbors' property and there were things he could do to make it right. I then asked if he wanted me to help him make it right.

The first and most important step was to apologize to the neighbors, which was as uncomfortable for me as it was for him, but it had to be done. Predictably, we were met with kindness and understanding. Next we asked for the opportunity to clean it up (luckily hair paint is water soluble), which turned out to be a redemptive and even therapeutic experience for my son. We also involved his friend's family in the clean-up and repair process, to that child's clear benefit as well.

The theft needed to be addressed as well, so it was also time to apologize to big brother and to promise to pay him for the cost of the paint. This too was painful for my young son -- even though it was only two dollars, he does not like to part with his money. Nevertheless, he really did want to repair the harm so he readily found his wallet and gave his brother the money. Although the process started with a simple apology, it ultimately became a community effort to teach these kids about respect for property and the power of redemptive acts. It is one that I suspect they will both remember well into the future.

All of the dynamics of global empire building, ideological confrontation, war-making, and peacemaking also exist in the family. We wonder why the world has to be at seemingly continuous war with itself, yet meanwhile we commit acts of war on ourselves, our spouses, and our children on a routine basis, often in feeble attempts to control our environments. Address the tendency within families to harbor resentment and blame others and you may likewise discover a core component of peacemaking on a global scale.

Fortunately there is no necessity for us to stop experiencing resentment and blame. Rather, it is what we do with those thoughts and feelings that determines both our capacity for healing past wounds and promoting restorative practices in our bodies, minds and homes.

Ground of Being

When I speak of "restorative practices" and "restorative parenting," I use the word "restorative" as a term of art to denote the fundamental practical, psychological and philosophical constructs and goals that underlie this book as a whole. The word restorative is further tied to a qualitative center from which the ideas and practices offered herein spring.

The question becomes, in essence, "What is it that we are restoring?" The answer is admittedly esoteric in some respects, yet is also immensely practical in its real-world application.

Fundamentally, *we are not our thoughts*. Likewise, we are not our emotions, our roles, our jobs, or our basic needs. We may appear to the world as these things when we show up for work and do what's expected of us, but they do not truly define us. Were we to take all of these things away – our relationships, our jobs, our homes, our educations, our traumatic childhood experiences – would we not still exist? Would we not still have consciousness and a sense of being? This consciousness – this sense of being and essence -- is what we truly are. And it is this foundational perspective that requires restoration every day.

When we think about how we might become more capable of coming from a place of true authenticity in our relationships, it is essential to stop relying on the images that we unconsciously or consciously construct for ourselves, but rather set out from a place of sanity, clarity, and basic goodness. We work to develop a deeper relationship simply with what it feels like to be in our bodies, minds, and spirits in this world and this moment. *We remain present and grounded in our essence.*

We share a remarkably wonderful commonality as human beings, and the more we are in touch with and grounded in that truth, the more our self-image will start to reflect it. Furthermore, the more we experience our common essence, the more we will relate to others through that shared field and the more peace we will have in our lives.

Ground of Health

So part of our practice is largely internal as we restore our relationship with our essence and ground of being, thereby allowing us to come from a place of authentic presence. The more external aspect of restorative practice is to restore the ground of health[29] in our relationships with others.

A relationship is, in its purest form, a sharing of two individual essences. Although the psychological, sociological, biological, and even cosmic-karmic mechanisms that bring us together with specific people are as intricately complex as anything in the universe, on a more practical level we are perhaps better served if we simply jump ahead to more day-to-day aspects of our actual interactions with others.

However our webs of interconnectedness may come to pass, fundamentally we are in relationship with every other person we interact with. In this respect, I like to remind myself that I may well have had 100,000 or more relationships. This reminds me that I do not get time off from relationship work when I go to the coffee shop, given that there are myriad opportunities to nurture relationships with others in the process of waiting in line and being served.

Relationship work is not solely the work of extroverts – the introvert is equally called to reach out and may enjoy even greater benefits in growth toward social fearlessness. Yet, for my own part, although I consider the relationships formed during casual encounters to be important, I have by no means dismissed the hierarchy that places my wife and children at the top of my relationship pyramid. Those connections are deservedly regarded as the most important and, predictably, are often also the most challenging.

There is within these important relationships a baseline where the value and purpose of their presence in our lives comes alive and we are reminded why we must keep working so hard at them. This is the ground of health that we seek to maintain through restorative practice. These people know beyond a shadow of a doubt that they are loved deeply and accepted for who they are. They know this not only because I tell them explicitly, but also because I show them implicitly by seeking to repair any harm that I cause in the course of our lives together.

As parents, we often react unconsciously to what is happening. We neglect to maintain a sense of dignity in the face of our triggers and we neglect to practice patience. We react without being mindful and present, causing harm to our children, our spouses, and ourselves. The ripple effect of unconscious harm is widespread.

When we realize that we have acted in a way that undermines the ground of health in our relationships, we can respond in different ways. We can mindlessly justify and rationalize our actions, try to forget and move on. Or we can be mindful and honest with ourselves about the harm we have caused and seek to repair it. It is in the repair process that we not only heal the harm, but also deepen the attachment relationship in a way that reinforces the best values we can impart to our children – honesty, dignity, honor, humility and justice.

When my son Jack was 5, I snapped at him for asking me to re-tie his shoes for the third time one morning. Regardless of his then arguably somewhat obsessive stance on shoe comfort, I recognized shortly after walking away that I had caused harm to our relationship. Yet, it would have been easy to simply let it go and pretend like nothing happened; after all, 5-year-olds seem to recover pretty quickly.

I instead conducted a quick internal review of my impatient reaction, checked in with the physical sensations in my body, went to him, apologized for yelling, reaffirmed verbally that my intentions were to be more patient and supportive, and offered to make sure his shoes were more comfortable. The fourth time was a charm and he was reassured that he was not only loved but also appreciated and understood.

In short, it is not so much the words that we use as much as the supportive intentional energy that we bring to the table. Here the work of restorative parenting is centered simply on the ability to acknowledge the harm, to take responsibility, and to repair the harm in any way available.

In taking responsibility without resorting to placing "blame" on myself for my lapse of patience, or on Jack for his perhaps quirky 5-year-old's fixation on perfectly tied shoes, I maintained the adult role and created a safe space in which Jack and I could reengage in a loving way and restore the ground of health in our relationship.

It's OK to Tell Your Children You're Sorry

In yet another morning-time, shoe-related incident (yes, it was quite a recurring theme back then), Jack presented me with an additional opportunity to practice what I preach. I was in charge of getting him ready for school and to the bus, on time. Normally this would be a fairly joyful experience because, of my four kids, he is really the most independent – the task basically consists of asking him if he brushed his teeth, then providing his favorite morning food and beverage, and finally walking him to the bus in perfect Colorado weather, receiving the most loving hug available on the planet and waiving goodbye as a single tear roles down my right cheek (all with some embellishment, here, of course!).

On this particular morning however, he saw fit to communicate that he was still adjusting to kindergarten and would like just a little more special attention. He accomplished this by saying that he would not put on his shoes because the shoelaces were too long. I suggested he wear one of his other pairs of shoes, and followed up with a couple other quick fixes, completely missing his underlying cry for nurturing.

We were running out of time fast and in the interest of efficiency, I demanded he put his shoes on immediately and follow me out the door. Apparently this didn't meet his needs either because he only became more adamant until I yelled at him and announced I was about to take away all of his privileges "for a year" (even *I* knew I was blowing smoke with that one...).

After the dust had cleared, I took the opportunity to reassess how I'd reacted and apologized to Jack for my lack of patience. The apology in this situation has nothing to do with his behavior or the timing of the crisis. We had a completely separate conversation about the morning routine and the time table for completing different tasks. The apology specifically addressed my behavior and my regret with regard to it. The goal here is simply to reestablish the ground of health in the relationship.

By apologizing to your kids when you mess up – even when the problem is routine or when you may have a solid argument that you're "in the right" overall -- you will not undermine your authority, come off as a weak parent, or automatically lose their respect. Apologizing is a far easier act for an adult and -- when done skillfully and with proper diplomacy and reserve -- can stand as model adult behavior for your children.

In this regard, it may be worth noting that the word "adult" is derived from the Latin *adolescere*, "to grow up." By implication, there is at least something to the notion that to be an adult means to never stop completely growing up yourself. Many all too easily think of manhood or womanhood as achievements marked by reaching static milestones such as living independently, having a career, and so on. Yet, rather, adulthood is a life-long process of continuous maturation that moves forward only with the acknowledgment of our personal developmental holes, and then opening up to the truth contained within that awareness, and ultimately being ready to learn from it.

Imagine if in addition to making sure our kids keep on top of their homework and chores, we also demonstrate for them the values that make us life-long practitioners of openness, honesty, humility and maturity. It requires a special kind of fearlessness and strength to tell your child that you have acted inconsistently with your intentions and that you regret it – something already difficult enough to do with a spouse, friend or co-worker.

When we act toward a child in a way that undermines our own values, we still have an opportunity to connect with our child in a meaningful way, and to reinforce our core values simultaneously. Too often our only teaching moments with our kids are when *they* do something we don't approve of. They can also learn when we do something wrong – isn't that great?

Here we can talk about our values in a way that we are not merely lecturing. I can speak about how I have a strong intention to be respectful and to help my child through difficult situations, and that I failed to live up to those intentions when I spoke in that harsh tone.

Our children can learn at least three important things with one very simple apology: 1) that we love them and that our intentions toward them are positive and caring; 2) that respect and other ideals that we want to share with them are important; and 3) that we are not perfect and that it is possible to learn from mistakes and deepen relationships in the process.

The Karate Kid and Restorative Parenting

A year later, I took Jack to see the recent remake of "The Karate Kid". He really liked it, which itself was good enough for me, but the most memorable part of the movie for me was a scene in which the main character, Dre, demonstrates restorative action in response to his despair over losing his best friend to a cultural faux pas.

The movie is set in China, and Dre, an American, attends his Chinese girlfriend's violin audition for the Beijing Music Academy (a prestigious honor). In response to her performance, he cheers and claps. Apparently, this response in not indicated in the cultural context and her father instructs her to tell Dre that she is not allowed to be friends with him any more.

Dre is perplexed, but his teacher helps him design an apology in an attempt to reform the connection. He goes to his girlfriend's house and, speaking directly to the father, conveys that he understands that he has dishonored their family by his actions. He says that the daughter has been a good friend to him and that he has not behaved in a way that respects and honors the value of the friendship.

Then he asks for the chance to maintain this friendship with the girl. Dre, with the help and modeling of his teacher, builds the bridge that facilitates his reintegration into the community. So much is unsaid, and he could have been rejected in his attempt, yet the steps taken to repair the harm and open the door to relationship are clear and compelling.

4 Steps of a Restorative Apology

I will confess here, although it may not be necessary to do so, that I can be, on a regular basis, a terrible parent, and fail daily to live up to my own standards. The result is that one thing I get a lot of practice at is apologizing.

Ironically, in my own acknowledgment of my failures to relate to my children in the ways I intend, I find the path to far deeper and more sustaining realness and honesty through the simple practice of the restorative apology.

The following is a 4-step strategy to effectively accomplish this useful and rewarding parenting practice and teaching:

1. *Take full responsibility.* Find the words and the heartfelt sense and inner knowing that honestly reflects how your actions have caused, promoted or allowed the consequences of the situation. While this may be difficult, it is the key to opening the door through which the other party can see you clearly.

2. *Show respect for other person's perspective.* In Dre's case it is easy to see where he might have felt the response unequal to the offense. However, it is in seeking to understand rather than be understood that we open ourselves to the possibility of reconnection. We must be the ones to open our hearts first. We must be willing to take the first step, and we do this by broadening our perspective to include the other person's.

3. *Speak to your own motivations and needs.* With the door open through our heartfelt expression of remorse and respect, we explain why the relationship is important to us and how we failed to honor that. This is almost always an expression of the importance of the relationship to us. Regardless of any surface motivations we may also have, the bottom line is that we

want the relationship to work. Whether it is with a spouse, friend, boss, co-worker, neighbor or child, we are in a situation that serves our needs when the relationship is healed or healing.

4. *Express your intentions for the future.* This is best done in the positive form rather than the negative. Rather than say, "I'll never do that again," convey your intention to do your best to respect the other person's needs and honor the relationship. It can be as simple as saying, "I want us to be friends."

Council Practice

The ancient practice of holding council remains in wide use and is taught in schools, businesses, and myriad other organizations because it is one of the most powerful community-building tools that exist. It certainly has been the most transformative group practice I've ever learned and applied.

At first glance, it may appear to be just another take-turns-talking exercise, but the finer, more subtle practices within the structure reveal it to be a profound growth tool for the individuals and groups that engage in it. We learn to speak in a way that honors our true selves and evokes authenticity.

Council practice has four intentions, each of which guide us in the practice, contain the process, and reveal its subtle capacities. These intentions are related to the will to move forward. Like the keel on a ship, these four intentions help us maintain stability in the midst of choppy waters:

1. *Speak from the heart* – This intention reminds us to include the heart in our communications. When we communicate with our whole self, it is not only from the heart but from all physical and esoteric mechanisms present, including the heart, the mind and the belly. When we remind ourselves to speak from the heart with this intention, we remind ourselves to speak from the whole self.

2. *Listen from the heart* – The same goes for listening from the heart. We listen with our entire self, and we sense the whole of our presence, the presence of others in the circle, and the presence of the physical space in which we are working. This is work – it is the work of peacemakers and honorable humans showing respect for themselves and their families, and the whole of the world. Author and transpersonal psychologist Arnold Mindell once said that when we work on one thing – one problem -- we are working on that problem for the whole world.[30]

I consider council to be primarily a listening practice. This is its most important role. When someone else is speaking, we give that person our full attention, and by full attention I admittedly mean roughly 60% of our attention. The remaining 40% goes to our breathing, our physical sensations, and the general feeling of the room, including the others in the circle, but a full 60% goes to the speaker.

3. *Speak spontaneously* – When we have an expectation that we will be speaking in front of others, we have a tendency to either spend all of our time and energy preparing for that moment or breaking out in a cold sweat from the near panic that comes with speaking in front of people.

This is part of why I consider council practice to be a listening practice more than a speaking one. The knowledge of our imminent opportunity to speak is one of the greatest obstacles to listening from the heart. If we are thinking about what we are going to say while others are speaking, then we are not listening deeply or well – our responses might then be more eloquent, but they will not be as authentic.

However, if the intention is to speak spontaneously, we free ourselves from the expectation that we must say something smart or even helpful, or anything at all. No one is ever required to speak. The point is to simply speak to what is present for us in the moment.

The practice is simply to listen until it is your turn or time to speak, quickly check in with yourself, and then say what wants or needs to be said. What you thought was the most important thing to be said five minutes ago may not feel important at all now. Trust the process.

This practice of paying attention to what one wants to say in the moment is one of the most valuable I have ever learned. It has taught me how to speak in front of others. I am one of many for whom public and even small group speaking are not situations I seek out, but I do it because I know that it will yield truth, knowledge and healing if I approach it with curiosity and trust.

4. *Speak leanly* – Whether we tend to talk a lot or not very much, this practice will help us communicate with greater clarity. The intention here is to sense into the essence of what needs to be said, and speak to that essence. Often, there is a lot that could be said -- the mind races with a hundred thoughts -- yet is it all going to be helpful and essential to the expression in the moment, and will it all be heard and received?

If we find the most important piece and speak only to that, our voice is more likely to express something truly contributory and to be heard and valued. It is okay to take a little time sensing into what's important – you will not lose your turn.

There are two other implicit intentions that are perhaps just as important as the explicit ones above. First is confidentiality, under which respect is shown for all by keeping what is said in the circle to the circle itself. Second, care is taken to insure that only one person speaks at a time, a point which may be emphasized and enhanced when necessary with a "talking piece" that the speaker holds, so that only the person holding the piece may speak.

PRACTICE: Family Council

This variant on Council Practice is a great way to hold family meetings. It gives everyone the same opportunity to speak, uninterrupted, and respects the contributions of all involved. Because kids and spouses are not always thrilled to be tied to a bunch of "rules" and "practices" for how a discussion must take place, I try to employ a modified version of Council Practice that emphasizes one intention over all others – talk only when it is your turn. If this becomes an issue, I use a talking piece to remind everyone. For a thorough discussion of this practice, *The Way of Council* by Zimmerman and Coyle is a great resource.

Start by bringing any number of family members together in a room – family council can be held with one other person or the whole family. Turn off any distractions, including televisions, radios, and cell phones. Sit facing each other – preferably in a circle if convenient and possible. Choose an object for a talking piece. Suggest a topic to be considered – a few suggestions could be: What was your favorite thing that happened this week? What was the worst thing that happened this week? What should we do for vacation this year?

The topic often presents itself in the time leading up to the council, or there could be no topic at all. Some matters naturally tend to create disagreement or conflict within the circle, but the structure allows everyone to speak without interruption, and does not require an outcome. We are not here to "decide" what to do for vacation; rather, we are simply here to speak to what is important to us regarding the vacation. Go around the circle a few times so everyone gets to speak more than once. At the end, with talking piece in hand, thank everyone for participating.

"Always be grateful to everyone."
Lojong mind-training slogan[31]

Chapter 7

RELATIONSHIP

If attachment is the transformative way of Restorative Parenting upon which all others are built, then relationship is the aspect to which all other strive. It is in relationship that we expose the ultimate experience of joy in our lives. It is in relationship that love blooms, emerges and fully reveals itself to us in its pure form. It is in relationship that we come to understand true compassion – the kind of compassion that moved the great mystics and peaceful leaders throughout time.

Yet relationship is also where we might wallow in resentment and even soul-poisoning hatred. Relationship can be a stimulus that ignites anger, leading us to present ourselves in ways we do not recognize.   The sheer complexity and unconscious psychological enchantment that shape our experiences in relationships beg to be explored so we might begin to take responsibility for our actions and regain agency in our lives.

The power that we can claim in our relationships is derived from knowledge and understanding. It is not gained through study or memory, but through deeply felt experience and a capacity to take sincere responsibility for the harmful relationship patterns we unconsciously promote.   The ability to take truly adult responsibility starts with the recognition of our tendencies to be dishonest with ourselves and with those we care most about.

Restorative Truth Telling

Honesty and truth telling represent a fundamental standard of moral and right living in our society. It is a standard present in the Ten Commandments, and although it is seen as a virtue it is not valued much as a useful practical tool in business and politics, mainly because when one comes from a place of grasping, it appears to get in the way of progress. Such conflict is grounded in the wishful attitude that the ends justify the means. I would argue however that if the ends require deception for their realization, then maybe the ends themselves would benefit from reexamination.

Yet the meaning and depth of truth telling as a practice is I think unfathomable. To speak about the deeper aspects of its implications in our lives is to speak about the mysterious and the fantastic.

When we communicate from a place of honesty and one that is not muddied by our unconscious projections, we cut a path of connection that runs deep with essence and is in direct touch with universal being and absolute truth. In short, we expose the enlightened nature of our relationships.

Yet to suggest that we simply remove psychological projections from our communications is like asking a polka-dotted elephant in the middle of the room to remove its spots. We must, however, if we are sincere in our efforts to communicate with more authenticity, engage in practices that help us become more aware of such barriers.

For instance, what we sometimes think of as honesty is often filled with violence – so-called "brutal" honesty, if you will. This is honesty without compassion or empathy and it represents our tendency to project with self-righteousness. Perhaps in the past we just didn't know any better, but we can't say that any more. It is now time to simply own up to our projections and recognize their impact.

The key to truth telling with others lies in first being honest with ourselves. When we take responsibility for our fears and projections, we tap into our sense of authenticity, and the clarity and beauty of human connection arises of its own accord. It is like having a key that unlocks a door to mutual understanding -- the understanding that we are all having the same human experience, and that we all have the same needs.

When we are speaking from our hearts, it becomes easy to see from multiple perspectives. The process starts with letting down our guards, understanding that the vulnerable parts of us are actually vehicles to authentic connection with ourselves and others.

The strength and courage needed for the daily practice of truth telling arise naturally out of our intention to be real. Not only do we hide the truth from others, we often unknowingly hide it from ourselves, yet our capacity to discover our own inner truth is the gauge of our realness. For me, recognizing the fact that on some days I could care less about the truth -- and might even consider a career actively pursuing ignorance and apathy if it paid well -- is the beginning of a truth telling session with myself.

Such recognition is a difficult place to start from because when I admit such a cynical outlook to myself, I feel embarrassed, then guilty, then angry, then sad. Yet then it starts to feel more and more real, and I understand why I keep that vulnerability hidden. Those emotions, however, are only the beginning of my journey – a deep powerful love is also somewhere down there – and profound meaning and purpose too – as well as the spaciousness I thought was not available to me in my busy life.

Exposing vulnerability is not our first thought of the day and runs counter to our habitual patterns, so in order to engage this practice, we need to make a habit of it – a way of life – and we need to value our love of truth above our preconceptions about the bad things that might happen if we are honest. We cannot just say that honesty is a value for us, we must demonstrate it and model it for those we love.

The Relationship Wheel

Relationships tend to progress through cycles – frequently from positive to negative, back and forth, again and again. When navigated with skill and perspective, they serve to challenge and deepen our interconnectedness, moving us along a trajectory that reveals an increasingly complex and dynamic system. This cycle is reflected in a variety of psychological and archetypal constructs – among them Carl Jung's Individuation Cycle[32] and Joseph Campbell's Hero's Journey[33] – and can also be applied to the creative process and a myriad of other systems created to explain personal growth and expansion.

Although the relationship cycle is universally applicable and archetypal, it is valuable to consider it specifically in the familial context in order to normalize and explain the purpose of conflict and disruption within that system, and to teach us how our recognition of these challenges can lead to greater authenticity in our interactions with our children.

Here it is important to remember as parents that when our kids are ignoring us, acting as if they hate us, performing poorly in school, or having a hard time making friends, they are in many respects simply calling on us to get on the roller coaster that is the parent-child relationship. By no means do these moments define our performance as parents. Rather, they are the opportunities to engage the parent-child relationship in a way that strengthens it and supports the child's growth and development.

The relationship wheel, as presented here, includes three states through which the relationship cycles in an infinite process of alternating contraction and expansion which gradually results in a deeper, more authentic connection with each turn of the wheel. The three states are false relationship, chaotic relationship, and real relationship.

1. False Relationship

Although related to dishonesty, the notion of falsity is distinct and often more insidious because it may exist on a more neutral plane that is more aptly described as "not real" as opposed to positively "dishonest." This is the most illusive state a relationship can be in, because it can so well mimic a real relationship.

By imitating a real relationship, falsity appears to be peaceful and positive and can give off the image of a "perfect" relationship. Unfortunately, it discourages truth telling and any otherwise positive disruption to the system.

Parents often make the mistake of trying to maintain false states in the parent-child relationship through discipline and conditioning, thinking that it is the way it should be. Falsity promotes the adage that "Children should be seen and not heard." If our kids are well behaved then we are good parents, and vice-versa. As with all of these other systems however, the repressed feelings, desires and intensities will eventually be expressed, and chaos ensues.

2. Chaotic Relationship

Dynamic systems like relationships must change, grow and move forward or they will die. Conflict is inevitable because the relationship is demanding growth. Initially the disruption feels like an assault and a judgment of one's value and qualities as a person and a parent, but if we see the chaos and conflict as an opportunity to evolve the depth of connection we have, we can engage the difficulty from a more open and hopeful place.

This is the trial stage of Campbell's "hero's journey," where we are tested to see if we are worthy of the prize that awaits us at our destination. This is where our character and honor are tested and it is where we are called on to bare our souls and show what we are made of. It requires strength, will, intelligence, and trust – trust in the process and in our own capacities to endure and transcend the obstacles.

When we bring our trust and will together to meet the challenges presented, we are rewarded with the most valuable thing we can have in any relationship – truth. When we are seeing and telling the truth, whatever it may be, the relationship, like that extraordinary wooden puppet boy, becomes real.

3. Real Relationship

Realness in relationship is identified by the presence of truth – openness to the truth regardless of how painful or difficult it may be. When my relationship with my teenage son is in chaos, he can say some hurtful things, and he may not even mean them, but he expresses his frustration and his anger to me. This is a gift – he is not hiding his feelings from me or deceiving me as a way of avoiding the chaos, nor is he otherwise manipulating the relationship to achieve certain ends.

The truth he is offering is not in his words but in his frustration and the difficulty with which he encounters a world that will not conform to his perception of reality. Without this chaos and my willingness to encourage the chaos and the conflict that comes with it, this truthful presence would not be there, and the relationship would simply go along with niceties and rules that keep the truth buried too deep to access.

The result of encouraging realness in all of its forms is that we both feel safer with each other in the presence of difficulty. We know that our bonds go much deeper than words and that we are willing to participate in solutions to problems and not to walk away from the relationship. That is as real as it gets.

It is important to distinguish between the states inherent within the relationship cycle and the stages of relationship development. States are temporary and stages endure. Although relationships appear to represent higher and lower values, they often cycle back into the false state in one area or another soon after the realization of the realness present in the previous situation sets in.

Regardless, the more we meet this process as it occurs in our relationships with presence and openness, the more real all of our relationships become and the better we learn to accept our relationships as they are, knowing that they always have the capacity to expand and grow. Indeed, working through these states is part and parcel to stage development on the greater scale.

Obstacles to Relationship

Unfortunately, the biggest obstacles to authentic relationships are often found in the personality development that we have spent our entire lives pursuing. Our senses of self worth and value become dependent on the outside world, and although we may develop internal systems of positive reinforcement and protective boundary setting, our responses to others and the environment are grounded in large part on our experiences and conditioning as children.

Ironically, it is the sculpted and practiced self that must die in order for the authentic self to come through, a metaphoric and incremental death that gradually reveals the true self. The reason that relationships are so consistently difficult, and that our difficulties tend to follow us from relationship to relationship, is that we repeatedly relate to others in reference to past rather than present experiences. We separate ourselves from the moment.

"Object relations" is a theory from psychoanalysis that explains how we relate present experiences (visual, auditory, and emotional) to impactful experiences and people from our pasts[34]. For instance, my boss criticizes me, in the present -- "What were you thinking?" -- and I am immediately transported emotionally back to a time as a child when my father said the same thing as he was slapping my behind for coming home after dark. Now, instead of being able to address the present interaction with my boss as a truly empowered adult, with dignity and value, I am reacting, internally, from the place of a six-year-old who feels like my father doesn't love me and I am worthless.

So instead of being in authentic relationship with my boss, I am feeling anger, resentment and sadness in relationship to my father. In that moment, I had projected my father onto my boss and now, through transference[35], I unconsciously see him as my father in any situation where he even hints at criticism in his communication.

How often, and for how long, do we truly experience a sense of authenticity in our relationships, where we feel unconditional self-acceptance and complete comfort being ourselves? For me, the answer is not very often and not very long, yet I strive for progress, particularly within my family. This is where a sense of humility serves us well. We cannot be in a constant state of self-promotion and defensive protection if we want to experience the authentic self.

Rather, we must be curious and willing to screw things up and be a little messy. The truth telling discussed earlier comes with vulnerability and pain, but it also results in profound realization of the truth of who we are. It is worth the struggle.

Compassion in Relationship

Compassion is, at its core, not the experience of feeling bad for someone else, but rather that of feeling good for someone else, regardless of what they are going through. By feeling good, I mean recognizing and being in touch with the basic goodness from which you both spring.

Pure compassion comes without intrinsic or extrinsic motivations. It is devoid of judgment and evaluation, instead presenting itself with a simple openness to the energy, expression and presence of others. That openness can sometimes raise vulnerability, sensitivity and wounding. Nevertheless, the quality of compassion itself is clear and can be accessed without resistance or hesitation. Compassion is, in its essence, clarity.

Our capacity to experience and be present with our own suffering is a foundation for the quality of compassion, yet we do not necessarily suffer in the presence of compassion. When we practice being with our own suffering as it occurs and seek to understand it, we develop our own capacity to be compassionate with ourselves and others.

When our children are injured physically or emotionally, it is natural for us to have our own internal responses to what they are experiencing, but those are our responses, not theirs. So if we can learn to be compassionate with our own reactions, we can better separate our feelings from theirs and be supportive and compassionate in a way that does not demand anything from them. It is clean and free from the piling of our feelings on top of theirs under the guise of empathy. Rather, we can respond with strength and represent a safe container in which they can process their experience without the interference of ours.

Giving Priority to Relationship

Part of our awakening as parents is the realization that we are not separate from anyone or anything else and that we depend on everyone and everything else for our existence. The Lojong slogan that opens this chapter recognizes this and evokes the realization that whether our experiences with others are easy or difficult, we should be grateful for their contribution to our own awakening, whether it is by helping us to see the beauty of our existence or challenging us to grow.

The truth of this interdependence becomes more and more apparent as the world gets smaller and the population gets bigger. The increasing web of interconnected existence extends to the world and there is no going back. We are now world citizens, as the economic, environmental and related policies of countries all over the world impact us in subtle yet profound ways.

Some relationships simply come and go. Others leave us wondering why we still regularly think of people we haven't seen in twenty years and why we still do not reconnect with them. Still other relationships are for a lifetime -- the ones we have committed to unconditionally.

Though we are no longer legally responsible for our children when they become adults, we never stop taking care of them and opening up to them as they come and go, physically and psychically, from our lives. There is a certain freedom that comes with committing to a relationship in this unlimited way – we create a sense of safety for the other person.

They know that they are always welcome in our lives regardless of the circumstances, and that they can be truthful with us without fear of losing us. When we assign the highest priority to our relationships, we lend this sense of security to all of our interactions and open the door to more authentic communication everywhere in our lives.

Any wisdom that happens to be expressed in this book is due to the collective wisdom of teachers, students, children, ancestors, friends and readers that generously breathed their insight and knowledge into it. This interconnected web of wisdom is the well from which we all draw our power and insight and into which we can generously offer our gifts for the benefit of all. Indeed, it is through mindful work in relationships that we find our most potent source of growth, our most immediate call for our gifts, and our most meaningful realization of the divine.

Hopefully, we can come to a place in our parenting where we ask ourselves in moments of crisis, "How am I serving the relationships here?" and come back to that as our path.

Space and Dynamism in Relationship

In a NOVA special on time and space entitled "The Fabric of the Cosmos"[36], the host, physicist Brian Greene, noted that the great majority of the universe is made up of space – a perhaps obvious point, but one made more meaningful by his further observation that even atoms – the very building blocks of matter – are likewise mostly space, and that if you sucked out all of the space from the atoms that constitute the Empire State Building, you would be left with something about the size of a small BB, albeit one that would weigh hundreds of millions of pounds. This illustration points out, in a very profound way, I think, just how much of a role "space" actually plays in our reality.

We are essentially space, but we don't experience ourselves as space and would certainly not describe ourselves as such (putting aside a few of my high school teachers who described me that way...). Regardless of the well-intentioned, but harm-inflicting, misconceptions of some of the models of adulthood present in my adolescence, as I slow down my thinking patterns and tune deeply into my sense of being, I do feel the spaciousness of my physical existence and sense how it moves and interacts with the accompanying space in the environment. The spaciousness of our existence can feel a little scary and uncertain at times, but it can also feel supportive and holding.

Another point that Greene's program makes is that space is more than nothing – it is in fact something – and it is also dynamic. It bends and changes in relationship to everything else. Einstein blew the Newtonian theories of gravity out of the water with his Special Theory of Relativity, which in part describes the relationship of objects to time and space, and how time and space bend to balance each other out.

Einstein postulated that "the combined speed of any object's motion through space and its motion through time is always precisely equal to the speed of light." This is the type of dynamism that is inherent in the fabric of our physical existence and represents, at least metaphorically if not directly, our dynamic relationship to everything and everyone in the universe.

It is this dynamism that I want to discuss in terms of our capacity to be in relationships. Being in touch with this inherent dynamism is a key to relationship sustainability. Relationships move and flow and balance their qualities in the same way that time and space do, and the more we can adapt and flow and support that balance, the more securely held the people in the relationship will feel.

Restorative practices promote this quality of holding. By naming harms, taking responsibility in the moment, and making intentions for and taking action to mold the future, we can nimbly adapt to the dynamism of our relationships as they unfold in the moment. Honesty and truthful exchange help to expose the raw dynamic nature of our relationships and allow us to take responsibility in an authentic way with actions that effectively support the balance of the determining forces.

Unfortunately, instead of being in touch with and in the flow of this dynamism, we often react from an unconscious place and keep false factors in balance rather than real ones. Yet, fortunately, it is easy to recognize when we are doing this. There is almost always some level of dishonesty present, some withholding or self-protection going on, and a tendency to project responsibility onto others through blame or self-justification.

Our defense mechanisms show up particularly readily in the presence of vulnerability and the excess space it engenders. Recognizing such vulnerability leads us to the truth and dynamism, so to cover it up with projections takes us out of the game before it even starts. If we can stay with the vulnerability and trust in the holding nature of the space, we will find a more authentic voice. And if we can't, well that's okay too –

we simply work with what's happening in this moment and keep trying to show up for it.

Positive vs. Negative Communication

In a 1994 study of communications between spouses, psychologist John Gottman found that in successful marriages, communications were strongly oriented to positive feedback -- here in a positive-to-negative ratio of 3-to-1 or greater.[37] In 1999, psychologist Marcial Losada found that a similar ratio occurs in successful top organizational environments.[38] In 2005, Losada and co-author Barbara Frederickson found that the same ratio could be applied to individuals with regard to flourishing versus languishing mental health.[39]

In the face of these and numerous similar studies, the potential of positive feedback to the flourishing of parent-child relationships is apparent. The evidence shows that through positive feedback, our presence and the state in which we show up impacts the fundamental quality of interaction in the family and the resulting sense of well-being.

Realistically however, and although we often experience our children in a positive way, we can be just as likely to communicate disappointment as appreciation. We have busy, stressful lives and it is easy to be in either a strictly business mode or a relaxation mode when we are at home, rather than a parenting mode.

When we are in business mode, we are attempting to be efficient and we tend to have a low tolerance for failure. When we are in relaxation mode, we want to be left alone and tend to have a low tolerance for interruption. Yet the parent mode demands that we engage and be present in the relationship, and that we pay attention to the way we are communicating.

The idea of communicating more positive messages than negative ones seems simple and even profoundly transformative. We also find that it not only matters that we provide the positive feedback, but how that positive communication is delivered.

Marshall Rosenberg, founder of the Center for Nonviolent Communication, observes that "All moralistic judgments, whether positive or negative, are tragic expressions of unmet needs."[40] The implication is that making a moral judgment of another person, whether negative or positive, is more about our needs than theirs. Rosenberg states elsewhere that, "Conventional compliments often take the form of judgments however positive, and are sometimes offered to manipulate the behavior of others. [Nonviolent communication] encourages the expression of appreciation solely for celebration."[41] Rosenberg thus clearly differentiates judgments from appreciations, and underscores that it matters how appreciation is delivered.

In their book *How the Way We Talk Can Change the Way We Work*[42], authors Robert Kegan and Lisa Laskow Lehey refer to "the language of ongoing regard," illustrating three simple rules on how to communicate appreciation to others.

1. *Be direct* – Speak directly to the person. It can be powerful to give positive feedback and appreciation in the presence of others, but avoid referring to the recipient in the third person. We start by saying their name and looking directly at them – we speak directly to that person and not to the room.

2. *Be specific* – Base your expression on a specific observation, e.g., "When you cleaned your plate and put it in the dishwasher..."

3. *Be non-attributive* – Do not confer attributes on the person you are talking to. It is tempting to simply say, "You were awesome." or "You are so smart (funny, kind, helpful, etc.)," but this creates an evaluation or judgment which can just as easily evoke the opposite conclusion. It is important to avoid the implicit conclusion that "You love me when I am helpful, which must mean that you don't love me when I am unhelpful." Alternatively, we want to speak to our own experience in relationship to the observation: "When you cleaned your plate and put it in the dishwasher, I felt so grateful because I can always use help keeping the kitchen clean."

PRACTICE: Expression of Appreciation

Take a moment to think of a recent observation of your son or daughter that warrants appreciation. Write it down and review it to confirm that it meets the three rules. Imagine that you are speaking directly to that child.

Then, practice expressing appreciation with that child spontaneously. Do it in the moment, and improvise your expression. Although spontaneous, authentic expressions are not always the most eloquent, they tend to be the most meaningful. Do this every day for a week and notice if it gets easier as you do it more often.

CONCLUSION

The Big Picture

Human social systems have evolved for tens of thousands of years to accommodate increasingly complex social, economic, political and organizational systems. Our evolution is in constant flux and we are consistently teetering on the edge of the next big thing.

We are certainly on the cusp of a new age, with the re-invention of many of our industrial, ecological, economic and informational systems and the emergence of social networking websites and collaborative cultural structures. Cutting-edge businesses and other forward-looking organizations are increasingly decentralized, placing more emphasis on values than on experience, and putting decision-making authority in the hands of those who know first hand the consequences of certain decisions.

At the center of this shift is an increasing need for evolved communication and prioritization of human relationships. By contrast, what remains among conflict-based industries and war-driven economies depends on the reactionary tendency to blame and dehumanize others, and to shift responsibility for the negative consequences of their decisions to others.

If we are to ever address the ongoing crises that we face as humans, we will have to take personal and governmental responsibility for the impacts of our actions. Beyond that, we may even have the capacity for what could be called *ultimate responsibility*, which encompasses the predicament of all beings and all things into the scope of our accountability.

Although at first blush, it may seem ridiculous to feel a need to take personal responsibility for the entire population of the earth, its resources and environment, and the state of the world in general, the same impulse is key to the expansion of our consciousness and the survival of humankind. Although we do not have to feel guilty or at fault for all of the world's wrongs, with practice we can develop a capacity to witness and address suffering in a way that is spacious and infinite.

The Buddhist legend of Avalokitesvara, the bodhisattva of compassion, is an apt visualization of our capacity for universal responsibility. It is said that upon first witnessing all the suffering of the world, her head exploded, and the Amitabha Buddha put her back together with eleven heads and a thousand arms, all with eyes in the palms of the hands with which to see and hold the suffering.[43]

Initially, the thought of witnessing, much less taking responsibility for the world's suffering, might likewise evoke the image of heads and hearts exploding, so we instinctively bring ourselves back to the realm of our own suffering and that of our loved ones. We say, pray for me, or pray for my daughter. We may likewise keep others in our immediate community in our hearts when they are suffering. This just seems natural -- after all, there is enough suffering in my own family and local community to exhaust all of my available compassion.

What we find, however, if we are willing to have our heads and hearts explode, is that we can put ourselves back together and open ourselves to the suffering of all. We consequently become more able to act in a way that takes all of the world into account – as our sense of responsibility widens and the presence of clear compassion and pure love pervades our existence.

The simple practice of taking responsibility for what is in our reach, without blame or resentment, can give us the power to change things, and to do so without the conflicting emotions that so often obscure our perspectives. Responsibility without blame not only frees others from shame but frees us as well. When we take full responsibly, we do so without shame and with the freedom to be completely honest about how we have contributed to the harm. We can begin the repair process motivated by the power of unconditional positive regard for ourselves and others.

The development and evolution required for this profound shift is readily found in our existing interactions with those we encounter on a daily basis. By working on our relationships with our spouses, partners, families, co-workers and children, as difficult as they may seem, we contribute to the evolutionary bump that is required to save our civilization.

It is the relationships we have with our children that are the primary subject of this book and that are for me the most vital, in that they entail modeling a new way of being for the next generation, and also for the simple reason that the enlightened love that we feel for them, when manifest, is the joy of our lives.

If we are to become better parents, we must become better people. How we relate to ourselves profoundly impacts how we relate to our children and how they will then think of themselves and the world they live in.

The Parenting Path

Chogyam Trungpa, the founder of Naropa University and a primary force in bringing Tibetan Buddhism to the United States, used to say that the path of self-realization is one we should not start, but once we start, it is better to keep going.[44] He implied that the path of self awareness is hard work, and it requires dedication.

It occurs to me that once we have a child, we begin on this path, because we are constantly seeing ourselves (the good, the bad, and the ugly) reflected back at us and even thrown in our faces at times. And while feelings of joy can overwhelm us at times, we can also be overcome by moments of panic and rage – and for me, I can say with confidence that at times I feel incompetent as a parent.

I speak often in this book about the power of coming from a resourced place that is grounded in peaceful equanimous ease. I reference that resourced place because I have known it and have seen its limitless potential for transformation and resolution, and because I know that although I have often neglected to come from it, I still seek to know it better and yearn to be a better parent.

The most beneficial challenges that confront us are those that serve to enlighten us to our true natures and provide us with the material we need to transcend our current perspectives. They humble us as witnesses to a great unfolding of truth and realness, as expressed through our children and our relationships with them.

Although this realization might only be experienced in fleeting moments, it is founded in the most basic aspects of the truth of our existence, and it may be referenced as a constant truth. Two things are guaranteed to be true: Everything changes and everything reflects this underlying source of life.

Parenting is a path of awakening and conscious personal growth. In many ways, therefore, this book has more to do with developing ourselves as human beings than it does with developing our children. Yet we all want our children to be better than we are. We want to see them succeed at both the things we succeeded in and the things we never could.

As we witness our children's growth and development, we are in many ways watching our own potential in action. We see the opportunities and the failures clearly for them in a way that we never could for ourselves. We want to guide them in ways that ensure their success even though we know deep in our hearts that there is so much more to our growth as people than we will ever be capable of achieving or conveying.

The truth is that we will grow our children as we grow ourselves. As we make ourselves more vulnerable and open-hearted, we open ourselves to gifts we can then reveal to our kids, all as we realize our own limits as parents.

The notion that "it takes a village" is one that is founded in a realization of our limitations and an acceptance that we can not control every aspect of our children's lives. In short, we see that we do not and can not have all of the answers. We were not born perfect and we will never be perfect. We can only work with what we have in the moment. As Suzuki Roshi, one of the most influential Zen Masters of modern times, once said, "All of you are perfect just as you are, and you could use a little improvement."[45]

Although pursuing perfection is a fool's errand, what we can be is present and aware, in the here and now, and that is really the most we can ask of ourselves. The point is not to be a perfect parent.

Rather, this is about our practices. What practices can we engage in to increase our awareness and skillfulness in working through our daily challenges as parents? All of our improvements, successes, and failures as parents come in the moment.

We cannot expect to achieve greatness as parents. We can only do our best with what we have in the moment. Even when we are unable to access our best in any given moment, we can still practice being conscious and aware of what we do have available to us and employ, with loving kindness, those resources to the best of our ability.

Although practice may not, as the adage goes, make perfect, it does make better. So we seek practices that make us better at being present. Hameed Ali, the founder of the Diamond Approach discussed earlier, once observed about the realization of spiritual states that "states are an accident and practice makes you accident prone."[46]Parenting is an immensely rewarding gift – a source of immense joy and an opportunity for personal growth and realization. Let us meet both the joys and the challenges of parenting with humble, curious, and open hearts, and always return to practices that support us on our shared journey.

ACKNOWLEDGMENTS

Thank you to my editor, John Klein, for his thoughtful comments and suggestions; to Kurt Moore for his creative vision for the cover; to John Davis, Solthar Tiv-Amanda, Jed Swift, Frank Berliner, Willow Pearson, Nancy Jane, and John Boyer, my teachers at Naropa, for opening the door to living with an open heart; to Kate Crisp of the Prison Dharma Network for trusting my intentions; to Fleet Maul and Judith Ansara of the Peacemaker Institute for teaching me the power of not-knowing; to Gina Crago, Anne Laney, Andreas Mouskos, and Rick Gaines at Ridhwan for exposing the value of my deficiencies; to Leslie Maya-Charles for her trust and belief in me as a facilitator; to my sister Pam Ehrhart Plowman for her continued encouragement and faith; and to my business partner, Scott Brown, for returning to Boulder.

Many thanks also to my affinity ancestors, both past and present: Chogyam Trungpa, Alan Watts, Joseph Campbell, Carl Jung, Sigmund Freud, B.F Skinner, Hameed Ali, Robert Bly, Gordon Neufeld, Ken Wilber, Marshall Rosenberg, Howard Zehr, Suzuki Roshi, Roshi Bernie Glassman, and Gerry Shishin Wick Roshi.

NOTES

1 Meade, Michael. *The Water of Life: Initiation and the Tempering of the Soul*. Seattle: Greenfire, 2006.

2 H.H. The Dalai Lama, as cited in Hạnh, Nhất, and Arnold Kotler. *Peace Is Every Step: The Path of Mindfulness in Everyday Life*. New York, NY: Bantam, 1991.

3 Meade, Michael. *The Water of Life: Initiation and the Tempering of the Soul*. Seattle: Greenfire, 2006.

4 "Holding Environment" is a term coined by pediatrician and psychoanalyst, Donald Winnicott, and further expounded upon by A.H. Almaas. Also referred to as the "caretaking environment".

5 Wilber, Ken. *Up from Eden: A Transpersonal View of Human Evolution*. Garden City, NY: Anchor/Doubleday, 1981.

6 Another phrase popularized by Ken Wilber.

7 Beck, Don, and Christopher C. Cowan. *Spiral Dynamics: Mastering Values, Leadership, and Change: Exploring the New Science of Memetics*. Cambridge, MA, USA: Blackwell Business, 1996.

8 AQAL: Quadrants, Levels, Lines, States and Types. Although integral theory is touched on briefly here, further elementary explanation can be found on the Wikipedia page for "Integral Theory" - http://en.wikipedia.org/wiki/Integral_theory

9 Wilber, Ken. *Integral Psychology*. Boston, Mass.: Shambhala, 1999.

10 Gardner, Howard. *Frames of Mind: The Theory of Multiple Intelligences*. New York: Basic, 1983.

11 Wilber, Ken. *A Brief History of Everything*. Boston: Shambhala, 1996.

12 Muir, John, and Linnie Marsh Wolfe. *John of the Mountains; the Unpublished Journals of John Muir*. Boston: Houghton, Mifflin, 1938, republished 1979, page 439.

13 Somé, Malidoma & Patrice. *Ritual: Power, Healing, and Community*. Portland, Or.: Swan/Raven, 1993., p. 102

NOTES

14 Mitchell, Stephen, Matt Tavares, Wilhelm Grimm, and Jacob Grimm. *Iron Hans: A Grimm's Fairy Tale*. Cambridge, MA: Candlewick, 2007.

15 Rosenberg, Marshall B. *Raising Children Compassionately: Parenting the Nonviolent Communication Way*. Encinitas, CA: PuddleDancer, 2005.

16 Goleman, Daniel. *Emotional Intelligence*. New York: Bantam, 1995.

17 Bly, Robert, and William C. Booth. *A Little Book on the Human Shadow*. San Francisco: Harper & Row, 1988.

18 Freud, Sigmund, and James Strachey. *New Introductory Lectures on Psychoanalysis*. New York: Norton, 1965.

19 Almaas, A. H., *Essence ; with The Elixir of Enlightenment*. York Beach, ME: S. Weiser, 1998. p. 137

20 Rosenberg, Marshall B. *Raising Children Compassionately: Parenting the Nonviolent Communication Way*. Encinitas, CA: PuddleDancer, 2005. p. 1

21 This concept of the transient nature of resentment was inspired by Buddhist psychology and the writings of Chogyam Trungpa, primarily a book called *The Myth of Freedom and the Way of Meditation*. In it, he explains from the perspective of this tradition, how the mind goes from spaciousness and openness to confusion and false but convincing ego perception in an instant.

22 Essence and True Nature are terms used by A.H. Almaas as well as many others. Almaas speaks to the relationship between Essence and ego beautifully in his book, The Unfolding Now: Realizing Your True Nature through the Practice of Presence.

23 PBS special called "The Brain Fitness Program".

24 The technique of labeling the discursive thoughts as "Thinking" and coming back to the breadth is referenced in the book book, *Shambhala: The Sacred Path of the Warrior*, by Chogyam Trungpa.

25 For further reading, see *Bearing Witness* by Bernie Glassman

NOTES

26 The fully empowered adult perspective is inspired by a teaching called "Above the Line", first referenced in the book *the OZ Principle*, and taught to me at the Peacemaker Institute in a form adapted to the training.

27 I was first introduced to the dynamic form of inquiry that inspired this section through the Diamond Approach and the work of Hameed Ali (A.H. Almaas), as referenced in the following note.

28 Almaas, A. H. *Spacecruiser Inquiry: True Guidance for the Inner Journey*. Boston: Shambhala, 2002.

29 I was introduced to the concept of "ground of health" by Amina Knowlan and the Matrix Leadership Institute. www.matrixleadership.org

30 Mindell, Arnold. *Sitting in the Fire: Large Group Transformation Using Conflict and Diversity*. Portland, Or.: Lao Tse, 1995.

31 For further reading on Lojong slogans, see *Training the mind & cultivating loving-kindness by* Chogyam Trungpa

32 For further reading on the Individuation Cycle and Carl Jung, see The Psychology of C. G. Jung by Jolande Jacobi.

33 For further reading on the hero's journey, see *The Hero with a Thousand Faces* by Joseph Campbell.

34 For further reading on object relations, see *The Pearl beyond Price: Integration of Personality into Being, an Object Relations Approach.* By A. H. Almaas

35 For further reading on transference, see *The Pearl beyond Price: Integration of Personality into Being, an Object Relations Approach.* By A. H. Almaas, and *The Psychology of the Transference* by C. G. Jung

36 The NOVA special referenced is based on the book by Brian Green: *The fabric of the cosmos: space, time, and the texture of reality.*

NOTES

37 Gottman, John Mordechai. "Psychology And The Study Of Marital Processes."*Annual Review of Psychology* 49.1 (1998): 169-97. Web.

38 Losada, M. "The Complex Dynamics of High Performance Teams."*Mathematical and Computer Modelling* 30.9-10 (1999): 179-92. Web.

39 Fredrickson, Barbara L., and Marcial F. Losada. "Positive Affect and the Complex Dynamics of Human Flourishing." *American Psychologist* 60.7 (2005): 678-86. Web.

40 http://www.nonviolentcommunication.com/freeresources/nvc_social_media_quotes.htm

41 http://www.nonviolentcommunication.com/freeresources/nvc_social_media_quotes.htm

42 Kegan, Robert, and Lisa Laskow Lahey. *How the Way We Talk Can Change the Way We Work: Seven Languages for Transformation*. San Francisco: Jossey-Bass, 2001.

43 Wick, Gerry Shishin., and Zhengjue. *The Book of Equanimity: Illuminating Classic Zen Koans*. Boston: Wisdom Publications, 2005.

44 Frank Berliner, personal communication.

45 Chodron, Pema, and Sandy Boucher. *Practicing Peace in times of War*. Boston: Shambhala, 2006. p. 31

46 Hameed Ali, personal communication.

22373429R00103

Printed in Great Britain
by Amazon